THE SUPERNATURAL IN ROMANTIC FICTION

First Edition 1880
Edward Yardley

New Edition 2019
Edited by Tarl Warwick

COPYRIGHT AND DISCLAIMER

FOREWORD

This interesting work is more a compilation of snippets of lore, comparison thereof, and an exhaustive list of potential secondary sources, than it is a coherent work in and of itself. Yardley has managed to compile a formidable number of short sections of folklore into these pages; a work perhaps more valuable as a springboard into study than for study in its own right.

The topics are profuse; several variants of basic mythology, the legendary materials of Arthurian legend, and of older works, as well as then-modern works which drew on the older. "Arabian Nights" and similar works entering the West in vogue at the time of this work being compiled feature heavily; many of the stories are from the East. A large proportion of the content within this particular work is more about connections between different works (from many cultures and eras) and comparisons of the same, for the sake of establishing a literary tradition.

For those genuinely interested in the occult, folklore ancient and modern is a necessary subject, and this is one of only a tiny number of books I have personally consulted that I would recommend as a good list of additional material to peruse for spiritual or historical reasons.

This edition of "Supernatural in Romantic Fiction" has been carefully edited for format and content. Care has been taken to retain all original intent and meaning.

THE SUPERNATURAL IN ROMANTIC FICTION

PREFACE

I have for several reasons abstained from mentioning the productions of living poets and poetical writers, but have otherwise attempted to make my work as complete as it was in my power to make it. I have used the word romantic in opposition to classical, and possibly have made the word unduly comprehensive by treating of all supernatural fiction, except that of ancient Greece and Rome; and even that I have occasionally noticed for the sake of comparison.

E. Y.

THE SUPERNATURAL IN ROMANTIC FICTION

ENCHANTED PERSONS

According to classical tradition, Epimenides, Cretan poet, and contemporary of Solon, was cast into a sleep, which lasted more than fifty years, and, at length awaking, was much surprised to find everything changed. The seven sleepers slept longer still. These individuals, who were noble Christian youths of Ephesus, fled to a cave to escape the persecution of the Emperor Decius. The tyrant walled up the entrance of the cave, and left them to be starved to death. They, however, fell into a deep slumber, which lasted one hundred and eighty seven years. Coming down to the time of Romance, we find the Emperor Frederick Barbarossa enchanted in the Kyffhauser. He sits before a stone table, round which his beard must grow three times before he can be disenchanted and resume his empire. Some shepherds once penetrated to this place. He drowsily said to them: "Do the ravens still fly round the mountain?"

They answered in the affirmative.

"Then," said he, "I may sleep for another hundred years." And he went to sleep again.

There is a tradition that some musicians once played before this enchanted emperor, and received each a green branch as a reward. All except one threw their branches away. This one discovered, after a time, that his branch had become pure gold. The Kyffhauser are also the scene of the enchantment of Peter Klaus. He was one day accosted by a man, who told him to follow. This he did, and was led into a dell, surrounded by rocks, where he found several knights (doubtless of the retinue of Barbarossa) playing at skittles, and never uttering a word. Peter, looking round, saw a can of wine, and secretly drank from it. The wine made him feel drowsy; he fell asleep and slept for twenty years. This story of course suggested that of Rip Van Winkle.

THE SUPERNATURAL IN ROMANTIC FICTION

The story of Ogier the Dane in some respects resembles that of Barbarossa. Ogier, who was a paladin of Charlemagne, embarked, when old, on board ship to visit heathen lands.

The vessel was lost, and all perished except Ogier, who managed to reach land, where he beheld a castle, which he entered, but had previously to slay two lions. After other adventures, he passes into a fair garden, and eats some beautiful fruit, which has the effect of inspiring him with a feeling of disgust, horror, and despair. Whilst he is in this distressed state, a beautiful lady clad in white appears, and tells him that she is Morgana la Faye, that she has watched over his career in life, and will take him to Avilion (or Avalon), where dwell King Arthur and others. She gives him a ring, which not only does away with the effect of the fruit, but restores his youth to him. She then takes him to Avilion, and puts on his head a crown which deprives him of memory.

He lives for some time in a state of enchantment and enjoyment, when she takes the crown away, and restores to him his memory. She then sends him back to earth, and he discovers that he has been absent for more than a hundred years. He does great achievements, and is on the point of marrying the Queen of France, when Morgana takes him away a second time, and casts him into a state of enchanted slumber, and places him in a cavern underground, in which he has since remained. It is narrated that a man once entered this cavern, which is supposed to lie under Kronborg in Denmark) and saw Ogier, surrounded by steel-clad knights, sleeping at a stone table, into which his beard had grown. Ogier, half-awaking, asked the man to stretch out his hand. The man put forth, instead, an iron bar, which Ogier grasped so tightly as to leave the impression of his fingers on it.

"It is well," he then said, as he let it go: "I am glad that there are men left in Denmark." And thereupon he resumed his slumbers.

THE SUPERNATURAL IN ROMANTIC FICTION

The story of Thomas of Ercildoune somewhat resembles that of Ogier the Dane. Thomas was carried away by the queen of the fairies, allowed to return to earth, and then carried away again. Other distinguished persons such as King Arthur, William Tell, and Boabdil, with his Moorish knights, are enchanted very much like Ogier and Barbarossa. The enchanter Merlin fell by his own art He communicated a charm to his mistress Vivien, the lady of the lake, who tried it upon him, and enclosed him forever in a tree or bush or rock. From that time he could never be seen, though his voice might be heard. A Spanish ballad, translated by Lockhart, tells how a lady was kept enchanted in a tree for seven years by the fairies. The O'Donoghue, an Irish chief, disappeared in old times into the lake of Killarney. Occasionally he reappears on the surface of the lake, riding on a white steed, and surrounded by a multitude of youths and damsels.

Among other enchanted persons may be briefly mentioned the Flying Dutchman, who, with his ship and crew, is doomed to cruise about until the day of judgment; also the Wandering Jew, who, on account of his conduct at the crucifixion, is doomed to wander about the earth for all time. In some places the sudden roaring of the wind is supposed to indicate that the Jew is passing. In a Slavonic folk-tale a magician causes his victim to be perpetually carried about in the air. Sleeping beauties disenchanted by a kiss or otherwise, or ladies falling into an enchanted sleep, when approached by their husbands or lovers, are not uncommon in romance. One of the "Persian Tales" affords a good instance of this latter kind of enchantment. In the "Arabian Nights" there are instances of persons being enchanted whilst traveling.

The king, in the story of the "Fisherman," reaches the enchanted Black Islands in less than a day; but, when these islands are disenchanted, he finds that it will take him more than a year to accomplish the journey, which he had previously made in a day. It will hardly be wrong to include persons carried away by enchantment with enchanted persons. An example may be taken from the "Mort d'Arthur." King Arthur and his knights once rode hunting in a forest. Arthur, King Urience, and Sir Accolon of Gaul, being the best horsed, outstripped the rest. They rode their horses to death, but found the hart they were hunting killed at the edge of a lake. Soon they saw a ship with silken sails approaching them; and in the ship were twelve damsels who courteously addressed Arthur by name, and invited the three knights into the vessel.

There they feasted them and gave them lodging for the night. In the morning King Urience, on awaking, found himself in his own bed at home, in the arms of his own wife, Morgana la Faye, who had caused the enchantment. King Arthur awoke in a dark prison, and Sir Accolon, when he opened his eyes, was lying by a well. It is a common trick of fairies to mislead a man so that he cannot find his way. Such a one will walk round and round a field, unable to find his way out of it. This misleading, however, is perhaps not properly enchantment The remedy for it is for the lost man to turn his coat or cap.

METAMORPHOSES

Melusine is famous among ladies who have undergone transformation. Raymond, Count of Lusignan, was hunting the boar in the forests of Poitou. He lost the boar, outstripped his train, and, whilst wandering in the forest at nightfall, saw Melusine, with her sisters, dancing by a fountain in the moonlight. Smitten with her beauty, he asked her to become his wife. She consented, on condition that he would allow her to remain secret and unseen every Saturday, They were married, and her desire to remain private was respected by her husband, until one of his friends maliciously suggested that she only desired privacy in order to indulge an adulterous passion. Raymond thereupon burst into her chamber, and discovered that the reason of her retirement was that she was doomed to have the lower half of her body transformed to that of a serpent every Saturday. The consequence of her husband having broken his promise was that she was compelled thenceforth to leave him forever, and be totally transformed to a serpent. Her spirit, however, continued to haunt the castle of Lusignan before the death of any of the lords of that race. Andersen's story of the "Wild Swans" affords an example of a transformation which had effect only during the daytime. At night the birds recovered their human form. As Thomas of Ercildoune lay on Huntley bank, he saw a beautiful lady, mounted on a milk-white steed, from whose mane hung thirty silver bells and nine. This was the Queen of Elfinland. Thomas, to purchase her love, swore to be her slave, and, after this, the appearance of the lady was changed to that of the most hideous hag in existence.

Alcina and others are beautiful, or hideous, according to circumstances. The metamorphoses, however, of medieval and modern poets are generally borrowed from the classics. To take an instance from the "Gerusalemme Liberata." In an enchanted wood Tancred gashes a tree with his sword. Blood issues from the trunk, and the voice of Clorinda tells him that she has been transformed to a tree, and implores him to spare her. This, of course, is a repetition of the story of Aeneas and Polydore. In the metamorphoses of Eastern romance a great fecundity of imagination is displayed.

In the "Arabian Nights" the King of the Black Islands had the lower half of him transformed to marble, whilst his city was changed into a lake, and all the inhabitants into fishes. The resolution of the Div in the introduction to this story into smoke is a very appropriate transformation; and one may mention as similar to this the change of the Undines into water in Fouque's story. The barber's fourth brother, who was a butcher, had a quarrel with a magician, who, to punish him, changed the body of a sheep, hanging up in his shop, to the corpse of a man, and thereby roused the indignation and fury of the citizens against him. There are, of course, many other metamorphoses in the "Arabian Nights;" but these will serve as specimens.

Fouque in his "Magic Ring," has a beautiful story of a transformation. The substance of it is this. On the Finland frontier the inhabitants of Finland were in the habit of practicing all kinds of horrid witchcraft. But immediately on the other side of the frontier line dwelt a pious hermit and his son. One day the son went out to cut wood, and, just as he reached the Finland boundary line, he saw a huge white she-wolf. He threw his hatchet at the animal, and wounded it on one of the fore-feet. He then drew his sword, and struck it on the head. It fell moaning on the ground.

Then he felt a sudden pity for the animal. He bore it to the hermitage, and laid it on his own bed. Whilst searching for some salve for the wounds, he heard a human voice come from the bed. He looked, and saw, instead of the wolf, a beautiful damsel, with wounds on the head and hand. She told him that she had been sent by her father, who was a wizard, to roam about the country in the shape of a wolf; and it was evident that the holiness of the hermitage had restored her to human shape. She is cured by the young man, and, a mutual attachment arising, they agree to marry. Before the wedding-day they stroll to look at the place where they originally met. They incautiously cross the frontier. They are at once surrounded by sprites and witches, and she is snatched away from him for ever. He pines away, and dies, and is buried at his own request at the spot where he met the white wolf. After his death the howling of a wolf, mingled with the wailing of a woman, was often heard at the grave. Men and women have frequently the power in romance of becoming werewolves.

This, for instance, is shown in one of the "Lays of Marie." In one of the "Persian Tales," which, by the way, are supposed to have some French additions to them, two handsome

Jinn are transformed by an enchanter into hideous old men, until they can find women who will love them under that form. There is a Persian tale, in which, by means of a ring, an enchantress takes the form of the Queen of Thibet. The King cannot tell the difference between the true and the false, and drives away the true Queen. This is a sort of transformation not uncommon in romance; nor is it unknown in classical fiction, as the story of Jupiter and Amphitryon shows. In the "Gesta Romanorum," an angel assumes the form of an emperor; and the real emperor is treated as an impostor. In the "Gesta Romanorum" also may be found the story of the transformed angel, of which Parnell and Voltaire have made use. This story is also in the "Talmud." In the "Orlando Innamorato," and elsewhere, a dragon is transformed to a lovely woman by being kissed on the mouth. In a Norwegian popular story, which has furnished materials for Count Hamilton's "Fleur d'Epine," a man with certain enchanted articles in his possession, and mounted on an enchanted horse, is flying from a Troll, whom he has robbed of these things. In order to stop the Troll, who is gaining upon him, he flings behind him his switch, which is straightway converted into an immensely high and long hedge.

The Troll, having surmounted this obstacle, still gains on the rider, who throws behind him a flask of water, which is transformed into a vast lake. By these means the horse and man get beyond the power of the Troll, without being overtaken. This sort of metamorphosis for the purpose of obstruction is in an Indian story; and it may be here said that very many of the folk-stories can be traced back to India. In a Swedish folk-tale a mermaid carries away a prince to her palace under the sea. She imposes upon him tasks, the execution of which would have been impossible had he not been aided by the mermaid's waiting-maid. At length the prince and the waiting-maid agree to fly together, mounted upon the mermaid's black horse and black mare. The mermaid sends after them, and, to elude pursuit, the waiting-maid changes herself and her lover, the prince, first into rats, then into birds, and finally into trees. Madame d'Aulnoy's "Bee and Orange Tree" is similar to this story. In the "Orlando Innamorato" Mandricardo plunges into a fountain, and finds at the bottom a lady, who directs him in the achievement of an adventure, whereby he obtains the arms of Hector.

In the performance of this feat he reaps a field of golden grain, when every stalk is immediately transformed into some furious beast, which flies at him. He also tears up a tree by the roots, and every leaf which he shakes from the tree becomes a ravenous bird of prey, which attacks him. As instances of semi-transformation one may remember Bottom and those enchanted by Comus. Parnell's poem, founded on a fairy folk-tale, tells how the fairies took the hump from the back of one man, and put it on the back of another. In a Swedish folktale, which is similar to many other tales, a rude girl offends a fairy, and is thereupon made three times uglier than she was before, and is moreover made to drop a dead rat from her mouth every time she laughs.

In a Danish, as well as in a German folk-story, a king and his daughter eat of some enchanted apples, which cause their noses to grow to a most amazing size. Their noses are not reduced again to a natural size until they have eaten of other enchanted apples of a different sort. Hauff, in a story of much delicate fancy, has told how a witch revenged herself upon a boy by making him deformed. The name of this story is the "Dwarf with the Long Nose." The witch is buying herbs, when the boy is saucy to her. She is determined to be revenged upon him, but, dissembling her anger, engages him to carry the herbs she has purchased.

They arrive at a ruined cottage, which, as soon as they have entered it, appears to be a magnificent palace. The old woman whistles, and she is immediately attended by a number of guinea pigs and squirrels, who wait on her with human intelligence. She makes for the boy a soup of herbs, and, as soon as he has tasted it, he feels drowsy, and, as he supposes, dreams that he is changed into a squirrel, and serves in the witch's kitchen for seven years.

He awakes, and returns home, but discovers that he has really been away seven years, and that he is transformed to a monstrous dwarf with a long nose.

ENCHANTED PLACES

The garden of Irem, in the midst of the deserts of Aden, was one of those enchanted places which were only occasionally visible. In the reign of the caliph Moawiyah, a person whilst seeking for a camel he had lost discovered this phantom region. Islands seem to be especially subject to enchantment. That island, over which Sycorax, and, after her, Prospero ruled by force of magic, should be noticed first. It is, however, unnecessary to do more than refer to it. The island of the seven cities was only occasionally visible. Don Fernando de Ulmo, according to Washington Irving, beheld this island, and spent there a space of time which he thought to be only a single evening, but which was really a hundred years. In the "Orlando Furioso" Ruggiero, on the hippogriff, alights on the island of Alcina the sorceress, the sister of Morgana. There he finds Astolpho, who has been changed into a myrtle. In the "Gerusalemme Liberata," Armida entertains Rinaldo on an enchanted island; but there is a beauty about Armida and her magic abode which is quite independent of the supernatural machinery.

The island of Avilion, or Avalon, was the enchanted country whither both Arthur and Ogier were carried. Sir Launfal, a knight of Arthur's court, was also borne thither by his fairy mistress. Sir Launfal's horse was so affected by his master's abstraction that it was for ever seeking him, even after death; since the phantom of the horse has been heard neighing for the lost knight. In the "Orlando Innamorato," Orlando fights with the guardian of Morgana's enchanted lake, and sinks with him to the bottom of the water. There he finds himself, as in another world, upon a dry meadow.

He renews the combat, and slays his antagonist. He then enters an enchanted garden, and finds Morgana, a lovely lady, asleep by a fountain. In a Swedish folk-story, a girl is thrown into a well. She sinks to the bottom, and finds herself in a beautiful meadow, and meets with other adventures. In one of the "Tales of the Alhambra," the Arabian astrologer sinks with the Gothic princess into a subterranean hall, and lives with her there enchanted through all time. He is, however, perpetually prevented from making love to her by the soporific influence of her magic lyre. In the story of "Aladdin and the Wonderful Lamp," the hero is taken by the African magician a long way into the country. They reach a spot between two mountains. A fire is lighted; incense is thrown into the fire, and magic words are uttered. The earth trembles and opens; a door with a brass ring is revealed. Aladdin is forced by the magician to go down into the earth through the door, and finds a subterranean palace and garden, full of enchantment and treasure. In the "Orlando Furioso" Bradamante is plunged into a cavern through treachery. She, however, finds that the cavern leads into a magnificent enchanted temple, which contains the sepulcher of the still-living Merlin. The priestess of the temple then shows to Bradamante in a vision all the illustrious race which is destined to spring from the union of that lady-warrior with Ruggiero.

A Turkish story tells the adventures of a Brahmin in an enchanted place in search of treasure. The name of the Brahmin is Padmanaba; and he, wishing for an assistant in discovering the concealed treasure, fixes upon Hassan, a young man of Damascus. The two leave Damascus together, and reach a well, which is filled to the brim with water. Padmanaba writes some Sanskrit words on paper, and throws the paper into the water.

THE SUPERNATURAL IN ROMANTIC FICTION

Immediately the water disappears. They descend by steps to the bottom of the well. A brazen door flies open, a gigantic Ethiopian porter is made motionless, and dragons, vomiting flames, are caused to retire, as soon as the Brahmin utters certain words. The Brahmin and his companion enter a subterranean palace, filled with treasure; and in the midst is the enchanted figure of a monarch, who had been a cabalist, and, by means of the philosopher's stone, had collected incalculable treasure. Padmanaba tells his pupil that the magical substance, of which the philosopher's stone is composed, not only transmutes common earth into precious metal, but also gives its possessor the power of seeing and commanding the spirits of the air. He also tells Hassan that it is by means of a cabalistic talisman that he is enabled to enter the enchanted abode, and rifle it of its treasure.

The tower of Toledo may be chosen as an example of enchanted castles. Roderick, king of the Goths, insisted upon entering this tower, although he was warned that, by so doing, he would bring evil on himself and on Spain. When he entered, he beheld the figure of Hercules, the builder of the tower, lying on a bed, with a writing in his hand. The king took the writing, and read it, and found it to be a rebuke on him for his curiosity, and a prophecy of the evils which would come therefrom. After a while, the king left the castle, and, as soon as he was come out, an eagle dropped a firebrand upon it, and consumed it to ashes. Then there came a great flight of birds, little and black, which fanned the remains of the castle with their wings, so that the ashes were raised in the air, and carried over the whole of Spain. And all those on whom the ashes fell were killed in the great battle which was the destruction of Spain. Enchanted places may be in the nature of illusions, and vanish altogether when the enchantment is undone, or the enchanter slain. The garden of the fairy Falerina, in the "Orlando Innamorato," vanishes when the enchantment is undone by Orlando; and only Falerina remains, all forlorn in the midst of a wilderness.

THE SUPERNATURAL IN ROMANTIC FICTION

MAGICAL SUBSTANCES

In the "Orlando Innamorato," Rinaldo, who loves Angelica, drinks from a magic fountain, the waters of which are destructive of love. Angelica, who had before been insensible to love, drinks from another fountain, whose waters inspire that passion. Huon of Bordeaux discovered the fountain of youth, which is supposed to confer perpetual youth on those who drink from it According to a later tradition, this fountain is to be found in Bimini, a fabulous island among the Bahamas. The water of death and the water of life often figure in folktales; and the elixir of life is to be found in other fiction. In the "Lay of Eliduc," a flower restores the dead to life; and a herb does the same in classical fiction. Hoffmann tells how Brother Medardus drank the Devil's elixir, and committed crimes in consequence. The love of Tristram and Isolda is supposed to have been caused by a love potion; and King Mark tested the fidelity of his wife by a liquor of another sort.

In an Indian story, Siva gives to a man a red lotus flower, which will change its color if his wife prove unfaithful to him. There is a shirt of like virtue in the "Gesta Romanorum." Oberon's flower, in "Midsummer Night's Dream," which caused love, maybe included among magical substances. Herbs are often used for purposes of enchantment. The mandrake, or mandragora, is a sort of vampire plant, that shines by night, and cries aloud when plucked up by the root. Those who hear it die, or go mad, as Shakespeare tells us. The mandrake is useful for purposes of sorcery, and it generally grows under the gallows on which a criminal has been hanging. The elder is a tree with magical powers. The elves are supposed to transform themselves into elder trees.

Hyldemoer, or Mother Elder, is an Ellewoman identified with this tree. The yew-tree is also magical. It has likewise the power of destroying magic. In a story by Immerman, a student utters a word, which reveals to him the secrets of nature. He understands the language of animals, and perceives life in what, to uninitiated eyes, appears inanimate. A magpie which he meets leads him to the place where a lovely princess has been thrown into an enchanted sleep, and bound in the meshes of a gigantic spider. The bird tells him that the princess can only be disenchanted by means of the yew-tree, which has the power to overcome all magic. He gets the yew-branch, but, whilst he abolishes the magic, does not obtain the princess. He, however, becomes sixty years older during the sixty minutes in which he gains his magical experiences. Oberon gave to Huon of Bordeaux a horn, which caused people not pure in heart to dance involuntarily. In the legend of the Arabian Astrologer there is a Gothic princess, who has a silver lyre, which has a magical power of producing sleep. In another tale of the Alhambra there is a silver lute, which has also supernatural power, but of another kind. A magic pipe piped away all the children and rats in the town of Hamel, or Hamelin.

Mozart has an opera, the subject of which relates to a magic flute. In that most disagreeable novel, "Sidonia the Sorceress," a Laplander plays a magic drum, and, whilst so doing, is gifted with the spirit of prophecy. In "Hassan of Balsora" Bahram, the Magian, beats an enchanted drum, whereupon camels appear, and convey him to any place whither he desires to go. In a story by Hauff the shipwrecked Said blows a magic whistle, which has been given to him by a fairy, and straightway the spar to which he has been clinging changes to a dolphin, which carries him away to a place of safety. Solomon possessed a carpet, which conveyed him whithersoever he desired to go. There are many carpets of this sort in Eastern stories. To Cambuscan were given four valuable gifts; a steed of brass, that could fly through the air, a mirror, that could discover falsehood, enmity, and adversity, a ring, that could make the wearer understand the language of birds, and a sword, that, like the spear of Achilles, could both wound and cure. A horse of equal virtue is to be found in the "Arabian Nights." The dwarf Pacolet, too, was the owner of a wooden steed, which had marvelous qualities.

One is almost inclined to place the broomstick, on which a witch rides among magical wooden horses. It is related of Charlemagne that he was once enamored of a very unattractive woman. When this woman died, he would not quit her corpse. Archbishop Turpin, suspecting sorcery, searched the corpse, and found a ring underneath the tongue. This he put on his own finger, when the monarch, losing his love for his dead mistress, became strangely attached to the Archbishop, who, thereupon, flung the ring into the lake, near Aix, which is the scene of the legend. But the sorcery of the ring did not cease. The king became so enamored of the lake that he built a palace on its shore, and spent there the remainder of his life.

The seal of Solomon confines Jinn, or Divs; and how this has been done is well related in the story of "The Fisherman," in the "Arabian Nights." The talisman for summoning these spirits is usually contained in a ring; and the fortunate individual, who possesses such a ring, has power over them. In "Aladdin" there is a magic lamp as well as a ring. To certain precious stones, such as agates, magical properties have been attributed, and the philosopher's stone is supposed to transmute baser metals into gold. Magic caps and rings, which make their wearers invisible, are common enough, The seven-leagued boots are mentioned in several folk-tales. Magic arms and Armour, mirrors, and the like, are too numerous in romantic literature to be particularised. In "Partenopex de Blois" the hero sails about in an enchanted self-moving bark.

So does Phaedria in the "Faerie Queen." Witches, too, can traverse stormy seas in sieves and in eggshells. Virgil makes brazen giants, which have a power of striking. Frankenstein does more, and, like Prometheus, makes a man that is possessed of life. Talus, the iron man in the "Faerie Queen," is borrowed from classical fiction. The wand and book are often the chief instruments in producing magical effects. When Prospero abjures magic, he says:

> "I'll break my staff,
> Bury it certain fathoms in the earth,
> And, deeper than ever did plummet sound,
> I'll drown my book."

Fairy legends tell of an ointment which, rubbed on the eye, enables the anointed person to see fairies, otherwise invisible. In the "Arabian Nights," Baba Abdallah becomes possessed of an ointment which, rubbed on the left eye, enables the anointed person to see hidden treasure, but causes blindness when rubbed on the right eye. Witches often smear themselves with a magical ointment, for the purpose of transforming themselves, or of taking their aerial flights. The divining rod is a means by which hidden treasure is discovered. The purse of Fortunatus was an inexhaustible treasure in itself, since it always contained money.

In "Blue Beard," a magic key reveals by an indelible stain of blood the disobedience of the wife. Readers of the "Arabian Nights" will remember an enchanted head, which speaks after decapitation. Goethe has written a poem concerning a magic broom, on a subject apparently taken from Lucian. The inexperienced pupil of a magician made the broom bring him water, but did not know how to stop it, and was nearly drowned in consequence. Hoffmann has written a story, in which an army of dolls is led to combat against the rats. Dolls are also animated in one of Madame d'Aulnoy's tales; and there is an indelicate story concerning an animated doll in the "Nights of Straparola."

Hauff tells how a student shuts himself up in a wine-cellar for the night, and is joined in his revel by a number of figures, who are animated for the occasion. Hoffmann has a story in which pictures are animated. The statue which accepted Don Juan's invitation to supper may also be put among magical substances.

When Bradamante is in the cave of Merlin, the priestess binds round her head a pentacle, as a safeguard against demons. The pentacle is also the instrument that confines Mephistopheles, under the form of a poodle, in the study of Faust. There are many other magical substances, such as rings, which confer oblivion on the wearer of them, or which change color, or drop blood, on the death of some absent person. There is a story in the "Gesta Romanorum" concerning brazen figures, guardians of treasure, which are immovable until the treasure they guard is taken, when they move, and cause the destruction of the robber. In another story of the "Gesta Romanorum," it is told how a necromancer, who is the paramour of a lady, makes a waxen image of her absent husband, and shoots at it, in order to destroy its original. A friendly magician, however, saves the husband. This story in its chief details reappears as the "Leech of Folkstone," in the "Ingoldsby Legends."

MAGIC YOUTH AND LIFE

A novel by Alexandre Dumas tells how a very old man, on the verge of death, has collected all the materials for the elixir of life, except the lifeblood of a virgin, which is necessary for the completion of the life-renewing potion. He has the barbarity to slaughter a young girl for the purpose, but discovers that she is not a virgin. As he has not the time or opportunity to sacrifice a fresh victim, he himself deservedly perishes. Faust changes from an old to a young man by drinking an elixir. Ogier the Dane recovers his youth through the agency of Morgana la Faye. Huon of Bordeaux discovers the fountain of youth.

THE SUPERNATURAL IN ROMANTIC FICTION

Ponce de Leon, a real historical personage, in more modern times attempted to make the same discovery. The water was said to be in Bimini, an island as fabulous as the water. It is perhaps not very surprising that Ponce de Leon was unsuccessful.

Classical fable tells us of Medea's restoration of Aeson to youth, and also of the trick she played Pelias. There is a Russian folk-story essentially identical with this fable. In a Hungarian story the dead are sprinkled with the water of life, and revive. In a story by Straparola the eyes of a girl are put out; but her fairy sister applies magical herbs to the sockets, and eyes and eyesight are restored. In a North German folk-story a man is deprived of his sight. A princess, whom he has delivered from peril, guides him. As they are journeying together, she observes a blind hare wash itself three times in the water of a brook, and recover its sight. She leads the blind man to the brook. He dips his head three times into it, and recovers his sight. Acts, to have magical efficacy, it may be remarked, are generally done three times. Thus Medea:

> Ter se convertit; ter sumtis flumine crinem
> Irroravit aquis; ternis ululatibus ora
> Solvit.

SPIRITS IN INANIMATE SUBSTANCES

In the story of "Aladdin," the spirits of the lamp and the ring are Jinn, who are bound to the substances, through whose means they are invoked, by talismans. Lesage has a dialogue between chimneys. In the "Adventures of a Guinea," a Rosicrucian has mental intercourse with an elementary spirit attached to a piece of gold, and compels it to narrate all its adventures in connection with the metal. Charles Dickens has evoked spirits out of bells. The lady whose life is attached to that of a tree in the story of Musaeus, is but a repetition of the fable of the Hamadryads, as old as Homer. Andersen causes trees, flowers, and the like to converse in a most sociable manner. Dolls are animated in stories by Madame d'Aulnoy and by Hoffmann. Hauff tells how a student shuts himself up in a wine-cellar for the night, and is joined in his revel by a number of figures, who are animated for the occasion. The statue which accepts Don Juan's invitation to supper may perhaps be rightly remembered in this place. So, in older times, did inanimate substances answer to an invocation. Ovid tells us that, when Aeacus asked Jupiter to repeople Aegina, which had been devastated by a plague, the sacred oak transmitted the god's assent by moving its branches when there was no wind which could cause the motion. Allusion may perhaps here be made to heads that speak after decapitation. It is said of Orpheus that his tongue still called on Eurydice after his body was torn to pieces.

In the "Arabian Nights," the head of the physician speaks to the king long after its separation from the body. In the "Mille et un Fantomes" by Dumas there is an instance of a lady speaking after being guillotined. The head of a horse speaks in a German folk-story.

CHECKS TO THE SUPERNATURAL

It is feigned that chastity is of itself a safeguard. Thus Milton:

> Some say no evil thing, that walks by night
> In fog or fire, by lake or moorish fen,
> Blue meagre hag or stubborn unlaid ghost,
> That breaks his magic chains at curfew time,
> No goblin or swart faery of the mine,
> Hath hurtful power o'er true virginity.

The appearance of morning is the signal for the dispersion of spirits, and generally renders them powerless.

THE SUPERNATURAL IN ROMANTIC FICTION

Then:

> The flocking shadows pale
> Troop to the infernal jail;
> Each fettered ghost slips to his several grave;
> And the yellow-skirted fays
> Fly after the night-steeds, leaving their moon-loved
> maze.

Christmas time, as Shakespeare tells us, is an especial hindrance to spirits:

> And then, they say, no spirit dares stir abroad;
> The nights are wholesome: then no planets strike,
> No fairy takes, nor witch hath power to charm,
> So hallowed and so gracious is the time.

The cross and holy water are sacred preservatives against devils and spirits, and can destroy diabolical illusion. Other holy things, like the spear of Ithuriel, have a similar effect. The pentacle is a magical preservative. In the time of Horace enchantments appear to have been undone by the reversal of a magic wheel; and the power of charms may be undone by speaking the words backwards. Boiardo mentions roses as having a power of destroying magic. He may perhaps have gained this idea from Apuleius. The yew is anti-magical. The guardian spirit in "Comus" produces a flower, called haemony, which he alleges to be of greater virtue than the herb moly, which Hermes gave to Ulysses. He says that it guards against all enchantment, and dispels all magical illusions.

The shield of Arthur in the "Faerie Queen," which resembles that of Ruggiero, has likewise the property of destroying magic. Running water seems to have a power against enchantment Tarn O'Shanter defeated the witches by crossing a stream. Rue and vervain, the herbs chiefly used by witches for

THE SUPERNATURAL IN ROMANTIC FICTION

supernatural purposes, were equally efficacious in checking sorcery, witchcraft, and diabolical power.

THINGS SUPERNATURALLY CONNECTED WITH FORTUNE

An English tradition tells how at Eden Hall a drinking glass was stolen from the fairies. They tried to recover their ravished property, but failing, disappeared, after pronouncing the following prophecy:

> If the glass either break or fall,
> Farewell to the luck of Eden Hall.

The glass has consequently been preserved with great care. Uhland has written a ballad about the luck of Eden Hall. There is a German legend concerning a tree, which flourished or withered according to the good or bad fortune of the country in which it was situated. In Scott's novel the White Lady has a golden zone, which increases or diminishes in agreement with the exalted or depressed condition of the house of Avenel.

SUPERNATURAL INFLUENCES ON THE AFFECTIONS

Hauff's story of the "Cold Heart" tells how there lived once upon a time a young collier, called Peter Munk, in the Black Forest. One day Peter goes into the forest in order to search for the good genius of the place, a dwarf, called the Little Glass Man. Unluckily he falls in with the bad genius, an enormous giant, named Michael the Dutchman. He afterwards invokes and becomes acquainted with the Little Glass Man, who grants him the fulfillment of three wishes. Peter makes a bad use of the wishes, and then has recourse to the giant, to whom he sells his heart for a hundred thousand florins. In consequence of his losing his heart, and having a stone heart substituted, he becomes a most detestable character. He is, however, saved at last by the good genius, and gets his heart back. In a story by Andersen the Snow Queen appears to a little boy as a snow-flake. Afterwards, as a stranger in a sledge, she carries him off to her kingdom in the Arctic Regions, freezing his nature, and causing him to be oblivious of his friends and relatives. From this icy tyranny he is rescued by a little girl, his former playmate. The influence of magical substances on the affections has been before noticed in this work.

TALISMANS AND SPELLS

In the "Persian Tales," Aboulfaouris, the traveler, met an Afreet outside a palace in a desert place. The Afreet asked the traveler to assist him in a little adventure inside the palace. He assented, and received a number of little leaden balls, which he was instructed to throw at the Afreet, whenever that spirit was overcome. The Afreet was likewise provided with leaden balls, and threw one at the brazen gate of the palace, which immediately opened. Two lions rushed out, but were rendered innocuous by the balls thrown by the Afreet. A second door was opened, and two dragons and two griffins dispatched in the same manner. The Afreet and the traveler then entered a chamber, above which rose a dome of red sandal wood. In the center of the chamber lay a man in a coffin, placed upon a golden sofa. The Afreet approached, and tried to take a ring from the ringer of the inanimate person, but a winged serpent flew down from the top of the dome, and blew on the face of the Afreet, who fell down insensible; the traveler, however, threw a ball at him, and revived hint The winged serpent breathed on his face again, and again the Afreet fell. The traveler was about to throw another ball, when the winged serpent addressed him, and said that he would exterminate him if he continued to help the evil spirit. The serpent then explained that he himself was a good spirit, that the inanimate body was that of Solomon, and that the Afreet was a spirit who had revolted against Solomon, and now wished to obtain the talisman, which would give him sovereignty over the world. The traveler thereupon desisted from his occupation of reviving the Afreet. Agib, the third royal mendicant in the "Arabian Nights," was wrecked at the lodestone mountain, which, attracting all the nails and iron in a ship, wrecked every vessel that came near it. Upon the summit of the mountain was a cupola of brass, supported by ten columns, and upon the cupola a brazen horseman, upon a horse of iron with a brazen spear in his hand, and talismans on his breast; and it was decreed that, when the horseman should fall from his horse, the mountain would lose its destructive power. Agib ascended the mountain, and, acting according to instructions, received in a dream, dug up a brazen bow with leaden arrows, whereon talismans were engraved, and shot the arrows at the horseman; whereupon the figure fell into the sea. Then the sea rose to the summit of the mountain, and a boat approached, in which was a man of brass, with a tablet of lead on his breast, engraved with names and talismans.

Agib entered the boat, and was being safely conducted to his own country, when, with mistimed piety, he began to praise God. Thereupon the figure cast him out of the boat, and then sank itself in the sea. The legend of the "Arabian Astrologer," in the "Tales of the Alhambra," which much resembles the story of "Avicenna and King Hormoz," in the "Persian Tales," deals with talismanic figures. Ibrahim, the astrologer, made for Aben Habuz, king of Granada, and fixed on the top of a tower, the bronze figure of a Moorish horseman, of which the magical property was that it turned of itself to any direction whence an enemy of the king was coming. Virgil is supposed to have made talismanic figures of similar virtue. In Beckford's "Vathek" there are talismanic substances, the writing on which changes supernaturally.

Perhaps the most celebrated of talismanic substances are the seal of Solomon and the buckler of Jann-ibn-Jann. The transition from the charms which are engraved or written, to the charms which are spoken, is easy. Abou Mahomed, the lazy, in the "Arabian Nights," exerting his magical power in the presence of Haroun Alraschid, moved his lips, and made a sign to the battlements of the palace, whereupon they inclined to him; and he made another sign to them, whereupon they resumed their proper position. In the "Lay of the Last Minstrel" the monk who met William of Deloraine in Melrose Abbey told him that he could speak the words that cleft Eildon Hill in three. "Open Sesame" were the simple words which opened the robbers' cave in "Ali Baba."

Spells are sometimes accompanied by acts, such as the throwing of water, the burning or extraction of hairs, and the burning of perfume. In the story of the "Moor's legacy" in the "Tales of the Alhambra," the spell was only effective during the time that a magic taper was lighted. Magic may often be undone by uttering a spell backwards. Witches exercise considerable power by means of spells. They can tear snakes in pieces with words. So they could do in older times, as Virgil, Ovid, and others inform us. They can also cause rain and thunder, draw spirits from their graves, and do other things by the same means.

MAGICAL ILLUSIONS

In Fouque's "Magic Ring" Tebaldo, the possessor of the ring, plays certain scurvy tricks upon the knight Folko of Montfaucon, who draws his sword, and tells Tebaldo to defend himself. Tebaldo laughs, and, by means of magic, causes to appear to the astonished vision of the knight not only one but many Tebaldos, all of whom jeer at him, and offer to fight him. The knight attacks them all, when a voice cries: "My pots! my pots!" and he finds that he has been demolishing the pots of an old stall-woman, instead of attacking his enemy.

There is something similar, but inferior to this, in a story by Straparola. In Hoffmann's "Pot of Gold" a student of Dresden is confounded by magical illusions, which are partly the work of a benevolent wizard, and partly of a malignant witch. The student seats himself under an elder, a tree notorious for sorcery, and hears the sound of little crystal bells, and sees golden little serpents, with beautiful eyes; and these serpents speak to him in a fascinating manner. He goes to the house of the wizard, but the witch prevents him from entering, by causing the knocker to wear the appearance of her own hideous face, and the bell-rope to seem like a huge serpent. There is a Turkish story, which tells how by force of magic a Sultan appeared to have lived seven years in a foreign country during a single second, when he was dipping his head into a tub of water. In Goethe's "Faust" the revelers in Auerbach's cellar are deluded by Mephistopheles into the belief that they are in a beautiful vineyard. The same magical illusion is in the "Richilde" of Musaeus. There are well told stories by Hoffmann and Andersen, in which, through the force of magic, a person suddenly seems to be living in a bygone age. In the romance of "Huon de Bordeaux" one of the enchantments of Oberon is the appearance of a wide river before the feet of the traveler. The river, however, is but an illusion.

The lake also into which Vivien carried the young Lancelot seems to have been a lake only in appearance. The Scandinavian fables also contain several illusions. In the "Lay of the Last Minstrel" the goblin page, in carrying off the young heir, causes himself and his companion to appear to the eyes of the guard like a lurcher and a terrier. Illusions are often practiced by the fairies. In "Midsummer Night's Dream" a fairy thus deceives a fairy. A fantastic tale by Hoffmann tells how, through illusion effected by a fairy, an uncouth boy gets credit for what other people say and do.

MAGICIANS

In the middle ages the poet Virgil acquired the reputation of a magician; and it is related of him that, having entertained the design of renovating his youth by force of magic, he made his disciple cut him to pieces, put the pieces into a barrel, and put a lamp under the barrel. The pieces were to be thus left for nine days; at the end of which time, if left undisturbed, Virgil would become young. Unfortunately the remains were disturbed; whereupon a naked child issued from the barrel, and ran three times round it, saying to the disturbers: "Cursed be the time that ye came ever here!" And with these words the embryo of the renovated Virgil vanished. Michael Scott, mentioned in the "Lay of the Last Minstrel," was obliged to provide constant employment for a devil in his service. He commanded him to build a dam across the Tweed; but this was done in one night. He then commanded him to divide Eildon Hill into three; but this was only the labor of one more night. Finally, he found constant occupation for the fiend in employing him in the manufacture of ropes out of sea-sand. Cornelius Agrippa was a magician of the middle ages, and the possessor of a magic mirror, in which he showed the fair Geraldine to her lover, the Earl of Surrey. The lady, although taken unawares, appeared to advantage, for she was discovered weeping and inconsolable for the absence of her lover. The magician used to be attended by a devil in the shape of a black dog; and this same devil, or some other, tore to pieces a curious and inexperienced young man, who secretly entered into the study of Cornelius Agrippa, and consulted his book. Reference has already been made to Merlin, Morgana and Armida; and Prospero and Comus are too well known to need more than the mere mention of their names. In a story by Anthony Hamilton it is told how Doctor Faustus exhibited to Queen Elizabeth of England and a select band of courtiers the spirits of famous and beautiful women. Helen, Cleopatra, and Fair Rosamond were successively summoned. Queen Elizabeth insisted on having the spirit of Rosamond up twice. She was, moreover, indiscreet enough to step out of the magic circle. Thereupon the spirits became mutinous, and burnt off the whiskers of the doctor and the courtiers. Magicians exercise a tyranny over spirits in other ways. In Le Sage's novel the devil

THE SUPERNATURAL IN ROMANTIC FICTION

Asmodeus is imprisoned by a magician in a bottle; and in a story by Musaeus a spirit is confined in a ring.

In the "Arabian Nights" there are instances of the subjugation of spirits and their confinement in vases and iron pillars. To know the secrets of the present and the future is also the office of magicians. Malagigi, in the "Orlando Innamorato," by magic ceremonies ascertains the designs of Rodomont and Ferrau; also those of Angelica. A distinction appears to be sometimes made between the black art and the harmless white magic. Thus too there are white witches, who only act benevolently.

WITCHES

When, in Ovid's "Metamorphoses" Circe, the poetical witch of the ancients, utters her incantation for the purpose of transforming the companions of Picus, the woods are moved, the earth groans, the trees turn pale, the grass is sprinkled with blood, the stones emit sounds, the ground is covered with serpents which issue from it, and ghosts flit all about the place. Doubtless this suggested the incantation scene in "Der Freischutz." Witches, both ancient and modern, made use of the cauldron. Medea, in order to restore Aeson to youth, puts into her cauldron, besides magical herbs, a screech-owl, the entrails of a were-wolf and other things. Canidia and her associates, in order to make a philtre, starve a boy to death. In the long list of substances, which are to be found in the cauldron of the witches in "Macbeth," are:

> Root of hemlock digged in the dark:
> Liver of blaspheming Jew:
> Gall of goat, and slips of yew,
> Shivered in the moon's eclipse;
> Nose of Turk and Tartar's lips.

THE SUPERNATURAL IN ROMANTIC FICTION

Hecate, in Middleton's "Witch," in order to compass the death of a person, puts into her cauldron marmaritin, cropped by moonlight, three ounces of the red-haired girl she killed at midnight, and other things. The ointment with which witches anoint themselves in order to travel to their sabbath is made out of the fat of a murdered child. The modern witches are generally women, who are supposed to have sold themselves to the devil, and, in return, to have the power of procuring pleasure for themselves, and of doing harm to others by supernatural means. They are thought to transform themselves to animals such as hares and moorfowl; and stories are told that these animals, after being shot and wounded, are seen to stop or drop, and assume the form of old women. These old women are traced to their habitation, and are there found in bed, suffering from a gun-shot wound. When a witch has a grudge against any person, she forms a waxen image in the likeness of that person, sticks pins into it, and sets it to melt before a fire. The original of the image, thereupon, falls into a consumption, and is afflicted with strange pains. In the "Gesta Romanorum" there is a story of a married lady who practiced witchcraft, in conjunction with her paramour, a necromancer. The guilty pair make a magical waxen image of the lady's absent husband, and shoot at it, in order to destroy him; but they are foiled by another wizard.

This story is also in the "Ingoldsby Legends." Witches are generally attended by a familiar spirit in the shape of a cat, and, accompanied by this animal, and sitting astride on a broomstick, they fly by night many thousands of miles. On Walpurgis Night they all assemble at the Brocken, under the presidency of Satan, who, on such occasions, generally takes the form of a black he-goat. One of the most innocent recreations at a witches' sabbath is the baptism of toads. Hecate, the ancient goddess of enchantments, has degraded into a witch herself, and figures as such in the plays of Shakespeare and Middleton. Perhaps she has fallen, with Venus and other deities, in consequence of the prevalence of Christianity. Lilith, who was the wife of Adam and mother by him, or, according to another account, by a Devil, her paramour, of a diabolical progeny, is the most distinguished of witches. She appears in the Walpurgis Night scene in Goethe's "Faust." The Scandinavian witches were in the habit of taking the form of wolves, and were then called were-wolves. We meet with werewolves in the works of Petronius Arbiter, Apuleius, and other classical writers.

DEMOGORGON

This is a being who apparently has power over witches and fairies. He is not known in classical mythology; and for this reason probably it is that Shelley makes him in his "Prometheus" the overthrower and successor of Jupiter. In the "Flower and the Leaf" he is mentioned:

> For cruel Demogorgon walks the round;
> And, if he finds a fairy lag in light,
> He drives the wretch before, and lashes into night.

Demogorgon is also mentioned by Boiardo and Ariosto. He finds a place, too, in "Paradise Lost," where he is the companion of Chaos. Spenser speaks of "Great Gorgon, prince of darkness and dead night." Perhaps he means Demogorgon. He afterwards mentions the name in full. According to a story by Voltaire, Demogorgon was the lieutenant of the great Architect of the universe, and to him was entrusted the making of this world. He was a being of limited intelligence, and to his blunders are attributable all the evils of life.

FAIRIES

These are supernatural beings in the Mythology of the North. They are generally of diminutive stature, but can increase their size as well as change their form. Oberon is their king, and Mab, or Titania, their queen. Shakespeare is their chief historiographer, but although the doings of the fairies are best illustrated by our great poets, it will be well to abstain from quotations which must be familiar to all or most readers. Oberon seems to have been known in the romances of chivalry before he was acknowledged as king of Fairyland. One old romance speaks of him as the son of Julius Caesar and Morgana la Faye; and it was he who gave the magic horn to Huon of Bordeaux, when that paladin of Charlemagne was on his journey to the East This horn had the power of making people dance involuntarily; and the Elfking's tune is said in popular tradition to have that effect. The Pooka, a malicious Irish fairy, which generally takes the form of a wild black colt, and does harm to benighted travelers, seems to be the original of Puck. For the two are similar in name and nature, Puck often taking the form of a colt, and misleading night wanderers, as Jack o' Lantern or Will o' the Wisp. In "Midsummer Night's Dream" Puck says:

> I'll follow you, I'll lead you about a round.
> Through bog, through bush, through brake, through brier
> Sometimes a horse I'll be, sometimes a hound,
> A hog, a headless bear, sometimes a fire;
> And neigh, and bark, and grunt, and roar, and burn,
> Like horse, hound, hog, bear, fire, at every turn.

The Elves and Trolls are also fairies. The Ellewoman is young and attractive, but hollow behind. All these fairies dance by moonlight, leaving after them circles of vivid green. They are generally invisible, and, when they are seen, are inclined to be malicious. They steal children, leaving others in exchange, and sometimes attach themselves to households. They appear to be held in subjection by the power of the Cross. A fairy popular tradition, repeated by Keightley, in his "Fairy Mythology," tells how a farmer once saw a bright insect, running restlessly backward and forward on a stone cross, apparently unable to get away. The farmer seized the insect and pulled it away, when it was transformed to a little black dwarf, or fairy, which had heedlessly alighted on the cross, and, because of the power of the sign, had not been able to free itself! The Trolls are possessors of treasure. They live under hills, which they sometimes raise on red pillars, when they are seen feasting beneath their substantial canopy above ground. Such fairies are not very distinguishable from gnomes. Goethe's ballad of the "Erlkonig," or Elfin-king, tells how a child was fairy-stricken in the arms of its father by a spirit which was invisible except to the child. There is a fairy legend of Ireland very similar to this. Parnell's "Fairy Tale," also similar to, and, in this case, undoubtedly founded on, an Irish legend, exhibits the power of the fairies, exercised somewhat less unamiably.

In the legend of "Thomas the Rhymer," versified by Walter Scott, we get a glimpse of the Queen of Elfland, who was clad in green, and rode a milk-white steed, covered with silver bells. In that poem, as well as in Hogg's "Kilmeny," which is similar to a German folk-story, we get also a glimpse of the mysterious and undefinable Elfland. An old Scotch ballad relates how Burd Helen was carried to Elfland, and rescued therefrom by her brother Childe Rowland. In the romance of "Orfeo and Heurodis" a strange compound of the classical and the romantic, Orfeo goes through a rock straight into Fairyland. The fairies of stories, such as those of Madame d'Aulnoy, resemble enchantresses. A common opening to stories of this sort is for the fairy god-mothers to appear at the birth of the heroine, and endow her with fairy gifts. One gives her beauty, and another gives her sense, but there is always one evilly disposed god-mother, who mars the beneficence of the others.

This wicked old person announces that the girl will be deformed if she sees daylight before she is of age, or that she will be subject to some other calamity. In the romances, such as "Huon de Bordeaux," the fairy ladies act in a similar manner. Some princesses in fairy stories have the power of weeping pearls, and dropping gold rings from their mouths. Others are less fortunate, and are compelled to spit toads and frogs whenever they utter a word. In the story of "Cinderella," the fairy godmother furnishes her god-daughter with an equipage out of very simple materials. She changes a pumpkin into a coach, six mice into horses, a rat into a coachman, and six lizards into lackeys. She likewise transforms the rags of the cinder-girl into a magnificent ball dress. In a Swedish folktale a Troll gives to a girl a pair of gloves, with which she can spin gold out of clay and straw. The condition of the gift is, that she shall marry him, unless she can discover his name. The simple Troll, however, himself reveals the name, which she could never have discovered. In a German story, similar to this, the name is Rumpelstilzchen.

JINN

Something of the following comes from the notes to Lane's "Arabian Nights." Jinn is the plural of Jinnee; and the Jinn are supernatural beings in the Arabian mythology. Sheitans, Afreets, Marids, Narahs, Divs, Peris, Ghools, and others, are the varieties of this being. Afreets and Divs are male and evil. Peris are female and good. The Jinn were created of fire thousands of years before Adam, and were ruled by a succession of kings, who were all called Solomon, the last of them being Jann-ibn-Jann. The Jinn are distinct from the angels, but the devils, or Sheitans, are the rebellious Jinn, of whom Eblis, formerly called Azazeel, is the chief. The Jinn appear most commonly to mankind in the shape of serpents, dogs, cats, or human beings. They become invisible at pleasure. If good, they are generally handsome, if evil, hideous. Solomon, the son of David, obtained great power over them. The male Jinn are said to carry off beautiful women, whom they keep as wives or concubines. The Ghool is a Jinnee, who haunts burial grounds, and feeds on dead human bodies. It is supposed that shooting-stars are missiles which the angels hurl at the Sheitans, who, when thus disabled by the missiles, sink to the earth, and become Ghools. It is related of Solomon, the son of David, that, on one occasion, he lost the ring which gave him power over the Jinn. An Afreet, named Sacar, obtaining possession of it, assumed the form of Solomon, and, driving him from the throne, ruled in his stead. The spirit, however, not being able to wear a ring which had the name of God engraved upon it, threw it into the sea. A fish swallowed it. Solomon, who, in his degraded position, had been forced to become a cook, found the ring in the fish, and resumed his power. In the admirable "Arabian Nights Entertainments" are many stories concerning the Jinn. "Hassan of Balsora," although by no means the best story concerning these beings in that work, is noteworthy, inasmuch as one of the incidents bears a strong resemblance to a German legend, preserved by Musaeus, and to other stories. Hassan observes a flock of birds flying to a pool near which he is concealed.

The birds, throwing off their bird skins, reveal themselves as beautiful damsels, and bathe in the pool. Hassan hides one of the skins. Presently the damsels resume their skins, and fly away, with the exception of the one damsel, who, through the loss of the skin, is compelled to remain behind. Hassan marries this damsel, who is the daughter of the King of the flying Jinn, and has children by her. One day, however, she recovers the bird-skin, and flies off to her native island of Wak-wak. There is an Indian story in the "Pancha Tantra" that a girl married a serpent, which threw off its skin, and appeared as a handsome young man. She burnt the skin, and the young man was obliged to continue in human form. A story, very much like this, is to be found in Basile's "Pentamerone." The Jinn, when on earth, seem chiefly to inhabit wells and ruins; but they abide also in the Garden of Irem, according to the "Arabian Nights." Richardson, in his "Dissertation on Eastern Manners," tells us that the residence of these beings was imagined to be the mountain of Kaf, which was supposed to surround the earth as completely as a ring surrounds a finger. The whole of this visionary country is called Jinnistan; and it is divided into many kingdoms and cities.

THE SUPERNATURAL IN ROMANTIC FICTION

Those of the Peris bear the names of Shadukam (pleasure and desire), Gouherabad (city of jewels), Amberabad (city of amber). The city of the Divs is Ahermanabad, and the enchanted castle of King Arzshenk is there. The Peris and Divs wage incessant war; and, when the Divs make prisoners of the Peris, they shut them up in iron cages, and hang them on the highest trees. Here they are visited by their companions, who bring them the choicest odors, perfumes being the only food of the Peris. The Divs cannot endure fragrant odors; and it is a custom to perfume dead bodies, in order to keep the spirits off. In a Persian tale King Ruzvanschad was hunting a white doe, which, on being pressed, plunged into a fountain, and disappeared therein. The king, believing that there was something supernatural in this, encamped on the margin of the fountain. He was awakened in the middle of the night by music, and beheld near him a palace, which he entered, and found therein a beautiful lady, a queen of the Jinn, who had fallen in love with him, and had assumed the form of a doe in order to draw him to the spot. She then took him to the land of the Jinn, and married him; but left him on account of his indiscreet curiosity concerning her. Among the issue of this marriage was Balkis, queen of Sheba.

ELEMENTARY SPIRITS

The beautiful fancy of Elementary Spirits seems to have been originated by the Jewish Cabalists, and perfected by the Rosicrucians. The Comte de Gabalis, in his discourse on the secret sciences, says that the air is filled with an innumerable multitude of people of human figure, apparently fierce, but really docile, who are called sylphs, or sylphides, according to their sex; that the seas and rivers are inhabited by undines, who seem to be chiefly feminine; that the earth is filled to the center with gnomes and gnomides, people of small stature, guardians of treasure; and that the salamanders and salamandrines, who are the most beautiful of all the spirits and the most rarely seen, are the inhabitants of fire. All these spirits are without souls, but can gain immortality by union with men, and then these unsubstantial beings become substantial enough. It is said that seven persons, fantastically dressed, appeared to the father of Cardan, and assured him that they were aerial spirits. It is a very common superstition that the gnomes often warn miners of approaching death by mysterious knockings. Hoffmann has written an excellent story, entitled "The Mines of Falun," in which he treats of the spirits of the mines. Rubezahl, whose habitation is the Riesengebirge, is a very famous gnome. Once upon a time he fell in love with a princess, whom he saw bathing, and carried her away to his retreat. To amuse her, he made her a present of a number of turnips, and gave her the power of transforming them into any shape she pleased. She sent him to count the turnips, which remained in the field, and, whilst he was gone, converted one of her turnips into a swift steed, and hurried out of his dominions. To count the turnips in a turnip-field is a laborious task even for a gnome; and, when Rubezahl had finished his work, and discovered the trick that had been played upon him, the princess had been gone some time. He hurried after her in the shape of a thunder-cloud, but she was already out of his reach. Rubezahl signifies counter of turnips; and his name is therefore commemorative of his simplicity. Number Nip seems to be a contraction of "Number Turnip," which would be the exact translation of Rubezahl.

The above story has been told by Musaeus. The Undines have a distinguished representative in literature. Everybody knows La Motte Fouque's story of "Undine," the wild, fascinating, affectionate water-spirit, who, after gaining a soul, by uniting herself in marriage with the knight, Huldbrand, is, through his cruelty, obliged to separate herself from him, and finally, against her will, to kill him. Upon her marriage with Huldbrand, Undine thus speaks to him:

"You must know, my beloved, that there exist in the elements beings who, in their exterior, differ little from human beings, and who only appear to them very rarely. In the flames the wonderful salamanders sparkle and play; deep in the earth abide the withered spiteful gnomes; through the woods wander the wood-spirits, who belong to the air; and in the seas and streams and brooks live the widespread race of water-spirits. Many a fisherman has seen a water-maiden as she was singing above the waves. Many a story has been told of their beauty, and men call them Undines. My friend, you see really an Undine before you. My father, who is a mighty water-prince in the Mediterranean sea, wished his only daughter to have a soul, even though she suffered as people with souls must suffer. But beings, like ourselves, can only obtain souls by the most intimate union of love with those of your race. I have now a soul, and it is you that I have to thank for it."

There is a very excellent fantastic story on the subject of elementary spirits in Wieland's novel of "Don Sylvio von Rosalva." Unhappily "Prince Biribinker," as the story is called, is more remarkable for its obscenity than for its other qualities.

Pope's "Rape of the Lock" is a very witty poem, but it is by no means a happy example of the Rosicrucian doctrine. There are other elementary spirits, which have nothing to do with the system as explained by the Comte de Gabalis. Shakespeare's Ariel is one of these. Of these too is the Neck, a river spirit in the mythology of the North. This spirit is sometimes seen in the form of a horse, at other times in the form of a boy, with a red cap, playing a golden harp. The Neck once questioned a priest as to his chance of salvation. Whereupon the priest replied, holding forth his walking-stick: "Sooner shall this stick bring forth leaves, than shalt thou obtain salvation." On hearing this, the Neck flung away his harp, and wept bitterly. The priest went on, but had not gone far, when he discovered that his stick was bringing forth leaves and flowers. He turned back, and showed the stick to the Neck, who, upon this, resumed his harp, and played away vigorously. Mermen and mermaids may also be classed among the elementary beings. The following is a legend concerning them. One summer evening a Shetlander was walking by the sea-shore, when he saw in the moonlight a number of sea-people dancing on the sand. Near them were lying seal-skins. As he approached, they flew to secure the skins. Then, clothing themselves, they were transformed to seals, and plunged into the sea. But the Shetlander had managed to seize one of the skins. He carried it away, and hid it. Then, returning to the shore, he beheld a girl, who was bewailing the loss of the skin, without which she could not return to her friends. The story, as may be seen, is similar to that in "Hassan of Balsora"; and it ends similarly. Spirits, like Sabrina and the Lorelei, who is supposed to be a stray Siren, though belonging to Romance, are formed very much after classical models. The same may be said of the wood-nymph, the mother of Libussa. Her life depended on that of a tree. The tree was stricken by lightning, and she died. The personification of the winds is classical, but Captain Marryat has written a tale in which one of the points of the compass is personified.

THE GOOD GENIUS AND THE EVIL GENIUS

Voltaire has an unfinished story concerning these beings. His story is in the form of a dream, which happens to Rustam, a young nobleman of Candahar. Rustam in this dream falls in love with a princess of Cashmere, and sets out for the purpose of obtaining the lady. He takes with him two favorite slaves, the one white and the other black. The white slave does all that he can to dissuade his master from the expedition; the other urges him forward. On his journey he loses them, and at the same time observes an eagle fighting with a vulture. Shortly afterwards he meets with a very fine ass, which he mounts; but the animal tries to take him back to Candahar. A merchant, however, gives him a camel in exchange for the ass, and Rustam resumes his journey to Cashmere. A torrent bars his way, but a bridge is miraculously thrown over the apparently impassable stream. Farther on he is impeded by a range of mountains. These open, and disclose an illuminated passage, through which he goes. He reaches Cashmere, but the issue of his adventure is disastrous. He is mortally wounded.

Then the white and black slaves reappear, with the addition of wings. The one, who is his good genius, tells him how he in vain attempted to dissuade him from an expedition which was fated to end disastrously; how he was both the eagle and the ass, and had obstructed him with the torrent and the mountain. The evil genius confesses that he was the vulture and the merchant, and had built the bridge and cleft the mountain. The idea that a genius attends each person, and shapes his destinies, is classical, and perhaps belongs more particularly to the Roman religion. A good or a great man may have an inferior genius; and then he has bad fortune. In "Antony and Cleopatra" the soothsayer bids Antony avoid Caesar, because the genius of the one is cowed by that of the other:

> Thy daemon, that's thy Spirit, which keeps thee, is
> Noble, courageous, high, unmatchable,
> Where Caesar's is not; but near him thy angel
> Becomes a fear as being o'erpowered: therefore
> Make space enough between you.

The Guardian and the Recording Angels are not dissimilar to the Genius. In a prologue to one of the plays of Plautus the god Arcturus says that he and other stars come down secretly among men in the daytime, and take note of their actions.

GIANTS, DWARFS, OGRES, AND MONSTERS

According to the "Edda," the dwarfs were engendered, like maggots, in the body of the giant Ymer. They live in the interior of the earth, and are artificers in metals; whilst four of them support the heavens on their shoulders. They are, however, of most importance in the fairy mythology of the North. Albrich of the "Nibelungen Lied," the original of Oberon, and Laurin of the "Heldenbuch" are dwarfs of great power in Romance. A yellow dwarf, who lives in an orange-tree, is to be found in one of Madame d'Aulnoy's stones. The giants are the constant foes of the Northern gods, and are destined, with the aid of the wolf Fenrir, and the serpent Jormangundur, to overthrow them in the end. Giants abound in romantic literature, but they seem to thrive best in nursery tales. Jack, the giant killer, slew a multitude of them with the aid of his coat of invisibility, cap of knowledge, and shoes of swiftness. The story of "Jack and the Bean-stalk," which figures in other folk-stories besides this one of England, contains a notable extravagance.

Jack's mother sows by accident some magic beans. In the morning Jack sees that the bean-stalk has grown up into the sky. He mounts the bean-stalk, until he reaches an extensive country in the clouds. In this country is the castle of a giant. Jack enters the castle, robs the giant of his treasures, and descends the bean-stalk. The giant tries to follow, but Jack cuts down the bean-stalk, and thereby kills the giant. Sindbad the sailor has an adventure with giants, so similar to that of Ulysses with the Cyclops, that the stories must have a common origin. In Wieland's "Prince Biribinker" there is a good description of a giant, who picked his teeth with a hedge-stake, and roared out with so dreadful a voice that more than two hundred crows, which had made their nests in his beard, flew out of it, cawing. The giant who haunts the Riesengebirge is Rubezahl, who, although a gnome, assumes occasionally a gigantic form. In Hauff's "Cold Heart" there is a dwarf, who, when angry, becomes a giant.

In one of the small stories of the "Arabian Nights" there is a story of an ogress. A prince loses his way, and meets a handsome lady, who conducts him to some ruins. She leaves him for a time, and he hears her tell her children that she has brought them a nice fat prince to eat. Profiting by this information, the prince immediately rides away. Amina, the wife of Sidi Nouman, in the "Arabian Nights" is an ogress. An ogre may be found in "Codadad and his Brothers." There are also ogres in the popular stories of "Puss in Boots" and "Hop o' my Thumb." Caliban is the son of a witch and the slave of a magician and his spirits; but otherwise there is nothing supernatural about him. An invulnerable sea-monster, with a prodigious appetite, is mentioned in one of the "Persian Tales," but the brute is disgusting rather than marvelous. In one of Madame d'Aulnoy's stories a princess marries an invisible husband, whom at last she manages to see, and discovers that he is a green dragon. This story of "Serpentin Vert" much resembles the "Cupid and Psyche" of Apuleius, and the Swedish folk-story of "Prince Hatt under the Earth."

Frankenstein manufactured and vivified a monster; and afterwards regretted that he had done so. There are some classical monsters in romantic literature which may be mentioned. Straparola has a story, which in some particulars is like something in the "History of Merlin." Straparola's story is nearly as follows. Constantine, who is a girl, disguised as a boy, takes service with Cacus, king of Bithynia. The Queen of Bithynia falls in love with her under this disguise, and, not obtaining any response to her advances, determines to be revenged on the supposed youth. She accordingly persuades the king to send him on the dangerous mission of capturing a Satyr. Constantine makes the monster drunk, and then has no difficulty in effecting the capture. The Satyr, however, is silent, except when he occasionally laughs; and the next labor imposed upon Constantine is to make him speak. The Satyr speaks, and explains to the king that he laughed, first because Constantine is a girl, and secondly because the queen's supposed maids of honor are really young men, and lovers of the queen. This revelation, so disagreeable for the queen, is followed by her execution, and by the marriage of the disguised Constantine to the king. A like story, apparently taken from Straparola, is to be found in the "Thousand and One Quarters of an Hour," stories which are called Tartar, but are really French. In this Tartar story, however, the monster, instead of being a Satyr, is a blue Centaur.

In Dante's poem the Centaurs are introduced as ministers of torture. Satyrs are to be found in the "Faerie Queen" and elsewhere. A Centaur, together with other classical monsters, figures in the "Orlando Innamorato." In the "Gesta Romanorum" and in the "Turkish Stones" are mentioned men with the heads of dogs, or birds, and other monsters. Some of these monsters are mentioned also by Pliny. Some monsters, such as the Questing Beast, the Blatant Beast, and the Ork, are altogether animals.

SUPERNATURAL ANIMALS

The story of the Phoenix, which is in Ovid's "Metamorphoses" is that it lives some hundreds of years, and, when about to die, burns itself to death in Arabia; and from its ashes a new Phoenix arises. There is always one Phoenix living, and never more than one. It is also said that, as there is but one Phoenix in the world, so there is but one tree in which it builds. Pliny says that the bird dies with the tree and revives with it. Sebastian, in the "Tempest" says:

> I will believe that in Arabia
> There is one tree, the Phoenix' throne.

The Phoenix figures in Voltaire's "Princesse de Babylone." The Simurgh is a wonderful bird of Eastern fable. It has the gift of speech, is as old as the world, and is invulnerable. It is a great friend of man and enemy of evil spirits. It has its habitation on the mountain of Kaf, and carries celebrated warriors on its back to combat. The Roc is another Eastern bird, but has nothing supernatural about it, except its size. It is, however, large enough to carry away elephants. The Hippogryph is a winged steed, on which Ruggiero, Astolpho, and other heroes, used to ride. The Griffin, half eagle and half lion, is a classical animal. Herodotus mentions how the Arimaspians steal gold from it, and Milton has remembered the passage.

The Basilisk slays men by its look, and may be slain itself by seeing its own image in a mirror. Perhaps the best description of a Dragon is that of the beast that the Red Cross Knight slays in the "Faerie Queen." He lay upon the sunny side of a great hill, himself like a great hill. He approaches the knight, half flying, half footing. A tremendous combat ensues, which lasts three days, and twice nearly terminates in the discomfiture of the knight. But in the end the dragon is killed. The Unicorn is another fabulous beast. Amazan, in Voltaire's "Princesse de Babylone," is mounted on an animal of this sort. So is the witch Dentue, in Hamilton's story, when she is pursuing Fleur d'Epine and Tarare. Horses are often possesed of supernatural qualities.

In a Hungarian story, similar to other folk-stories, Argilus bears away his wife, Helen, from the power of Holofernes, the fire king, who has carried her to his subterranean abode. Holofernes, however, has a wonderful horse, called Taigarot, who can speak, and has, like Sleipner, the horse of Odin, an unnatural number of legs. This horse informs his master of the abduction of Helen, and, being a horse of wonderful speed, he and his master soon come up with the fugitives; and Helen is recaptured. Argilus hears of a horse which is younger brother to Taigarot, and even swifter than that animal, although possessing only four legs. This horse is kept underground by the witch Ironnose; and Argilus enters into her service, in order to obtain the horse. His first duty is to keep in control the witch's stud of brazen horses; his next duty to look after the witch's twelve black mares, who are her daughters; and his third to milk the mares, and make a bath of their milk. All these labors he accomplishes with the aid of a magic staff, and obtains the horse, whilst the witch burns herself to death in the bath, under the impression that she will make herself young. Then says the horse to Argilus: "Wash me in the bath." Argilus does so; and the horse becomes of a beautiful golden color, and from every hair of his body hangs a little golden bell.

Upon this wonderful steed Argilus carries away his wife. Holofernes, on Taigarot, hastens after them, but, not being able to overtake them, digs his spurs into Taigarot, who, thereupon, kicks him off, and Holofernes, falling, breaks his neck. The above story is from the collection made by Mailath. In one or two stories an enchanted horse, that can talk, and give advice, after carrying its rider out of great peril, requests him to cut off its head. This apparently ungrateful act is performed; and the horse recovers its original human form, which in one story is that of a princess, in another that of a prince. It may be remembered that Madame d'Aulnoy's "White Cat" is disenchanted in a like manner. So in the Indian mythology Rama delivers a monster from enchantment, by cutting its arms off, and restores him to his former beauty.

In Anthony Hamilton's story of "Fleur d'Epine," the chief incidents of which are evidently taken from folk-tales, Tarare, mounted on the mare Sonnante, flies from the sorceress Dentue. Sonnante is a marvelous mare, from every hair of whose body hangs a little golden bell. The sorceress pursues them, mounted on an unicorn, and accompanied by two huge tigers. Tarare, however, takes a little stone out of the left ear of the mare, and throws it behind him, when the stone immediately becomes a long wall sixty feet high. The sorceress surmounts the wall, and gains upon the fugitives. Tarare then takes a drop of water out of the right ear of the mare, and throws it behind him, when it becomes a rapid and wide river. This last obstacle stops the sorceress.

In the story of the third royal mendicant in the "Arabian

Nights," Agib, with unfortunate curiosity, enters a room which he has been forbidden to enter. He finds there a black horse, which he mounts. As soon as he has mounted, he perceives that the horse has wings. The horse flies away, alights at some distant spot, kicks Agib off, and with a wisk of its tail puts his eye out. Many supernatural animals are human beings, transformed for a time, retaining faculty of speech, and often gifted with magical power. "The Chronicle of Three Sisters" by Musaeus deals with such animals. This is a charming story, of which the chief incidents are drawn from Northern folk-tales. The substance of the story is as follows. A count, who has three daughters, goes into an enchanted forest, and meets a bear, who speaks to him, and says that he will kill him if he does not give to him in marriage his eldest daughter. To save his own life, the count readily engages his daughter to the bear, who, assuming a human form, carries off his betrothed. In like manner are the other two daughters engaged to an eagle and a fish, and in like manner do these monsters assume a human form in order to be married. After many years the young son of the count goes into the enchanted forest to seek after his sisters. He at first is very nearly devoured by his brother-in-law, the bear, who, when in this form, is obliged to act like a beast. On one day in the week, however, he is disenchanted, and recovers human form. He then receives his wife's brother very courteously, and, dismissing him before his next transformation, gives him the three hairs of a bear, and promises to come to his assistance on these hairs being rubbed. Under similar circumstances does the young count visit his other brothers-in-law, the eagle and the fish, and receive from them respectively the gifts of three feathers and three scales. The three gifts are very useful to the young count, who, by their means, is saved from peril, and succeeds in altogether disenchanting his brothers in law. The above is not only similar to folk-tales undoubtedly Northern, but resembles also very strongly a story in Basile's "Pentamerone." A popular story prevalent throughout Europe tells how a princess, betrothed to a king, is changed by her step-mother to a duck. The bird comes by night to visit her betrothed, and in human voice, which she still retains, laments her fate. Her betrothed sheds three drops of her blood, and restores her to her original form. Anthony Hamilton's exquisite story of "Le Belier," treats of the enchantment of a prince, who is changed into a ram, but has power of speech, and is otherwise extraordinarily endowed. The princess who loves him, and is loved by him, stabs him under the impression that she is slaying her enemy. All, however, comes right in the end. With other supernatural animals should be mentioned Puss in Boots, the wonderful cat, which can speak, and is so wise that it makes the fortune of its master. In a story by Musaeus there is a hen that lays golden eggs; and in a fable, attributed to Aesop, there is a goose of the same sort. The white cat in Madame d'Aulnoy's story of that name is an enchanted princess. This cat, who can speak, persuades a prince to cut off her head and tail. She then recovers her human form. This story reminds one of the German folk-tale, the "Frog Bride" (to be found in Grimm's collection), and of the Swedish folk-tale, the "Enchanted Toad" (to be found in Thorpe's "Yule Tide Stories.") In some particulars it also resembles "Ahmed and Paribanou."

In another story by Madame d'Aulnoy a prince is transformed into a blue bird. After his restoration to human form, being persuaded that his true love, Florine, has behaved badly to him, he allows himself to be betrothed to his false love. Florine bribes her rival with magic gifts to allow her to spend a night in the room adjoining that of the prince, and, when there, tells him that she has been slandered, and that she is, and has always been his true love. He does not answer her, and she is in despair, not knowing that he has been drugged with opium, and cannot hear her. At length she ascertains the cause of his silence, and finds means to make him hear her. This story, in the above-mentioned particulars, is similar to "Pintosmalto" in Basile's "Pentamerone," also to the concluding part of "Prince Hatt under the Earth," and to the old German version of "Beauty and the Beast," in which the beast is a lion. This German folk-story seems to be identical with "Prince Hatt," except at in one story the enchanted prince is invisible, in the other he is converted into a beast. "Prince Hatt," which is to be found in Thorpe's "Yule Tide Stories," is the connecting link between "Cupid and Psyche" and "Beauty and the Beast."

Lamia, Melusine, the lover in the Indian story, the Peri in the "Arabian Nights," are all examples of supernatural beings, who are serpents, or have the power of becoming so. The Kraken and the Sea-serpent are supernatural on account of their size, the former being supposed to be miles long and miles broad. There is no reason why either should be supernatural, if reduced to moderate dimensions. Most of Prince Biribinker's adventures take place in the belly of an enormous whale. Fairy traditions tell of porpoises and seals, which assume a human shape. In a story by Straparola there is thunny, which speaks to its captor, and does him supernatural services. In another story by Straparola the hero is implored by a dying fish to throw it into the water. He does so, and the fish gives to him three of its scales, and promises to help him whenever the scales are laid on the bank of the river. In "Dornroschen" and the "Fair One with the Golden Locks," there is a similar incident. Animals, which speak in fable and romance, and conduct themselves humanly, but otherwise are not supernatural, need not be especially noticed.

THE LANGUAGE OF ANIMALS

A knowledge of the language of animals is not uncommon in romance. Sigurd, the awakener of Brunhild, understood the speech of birds. The following story by Straparola is nearly identical with one in the "Arabian Nights," and also with a Slavonic folk-story. A young man, named Frederic, understood the language of animals. The communication, however, of any knowledge, thus obtained, was to cost him his life. One day he heard a conversation between a mare and her foal, and smiled at what he heard. His wife insisted on knowing what he was smiling about, notwithstanding his assertion that it would cost him his life to let her know. He was on the point of telling her, when he heard a conversation between his dog and a cock.

"What!" said the dog to the cock, "can you crow when our master is about to die?"

"More fool he," replied the cock. "I can keep my hundred wives in order; and he is going to die in this silly way because he cannot keep one in order."

On hearing this, Frederic, instead of telling his wife the secret, gave her a severe beating.

The pretty story of the "Pilgrim of Love" in the "Tales of the Alhambra" turns upon the language of birds. Eben Bonabben taught his pupil this language, and thereby discovered to him the secret he wished to hide from him. In one of Hauffs stories the caliph, who changes himself into a stork, can, when so transformed, understand the language of animals.

THE CLASSICS IN CONNECTION WITH ROMANCE

Lamia, as a woman united to the man she loved and then compelled to resume her form as a serpent, and Derceto, half fish, half woman, haunting the waters of Babylon, certainly remind one of the later tradition concerning Melusine. Perseus, rescuing Andromeda, and Ruggiero, rescuing Angelica, are almost identical. Clorinda's story is the same as that of Polydore. Philinnium finds her parallel in modern fiction. Lucian's marvelous voyages and adventures inside a whale have been imitated in later times. The story of the Phoenix, how it burns itself to death, and how the new bird rises from its ashes, a favorite theme in romance, is told also by Ovid. The spells and enchantments of Circe and Medea have often been renewed in literature, with variations. The magic and witchcraft of Thessaly, described by Apuleius in his "Golden Ass" are not unlike the magic and witchcraft of a later time. His story of "Psyche and Cupid" bears a resemblance to more than one folk-story. Other resemblances between the classical and romantic stories might be remarked. Both Alpheus, the river god, and Kuhleborn, in "Undine" change themselves from the form and substance of man into water at will. Rhoecus prevents a tree from being cut down, and thus preserves the life of a wood-nymph, whose existence depends upon that of the tree. Similarly is the mother of Libussa saved from destruction. Minerva, in transforming Arachne, sprinkles her with a magical fluid, very much as an Arabian enchantress would have done, though the latter would have used water for the purpose. The helmet of Pluto, which rendered its wearer invisible, is similar to the cap in many fairy tales. The spear of Achilles, which cured those it hurt, reminds one of a sword mentioned by Chaucer.

In the history of Huon de Bordeaux there is a magic goblet, which spontaneously fills with wine. Ovid, in the story of Philemon and Baucis, tells how the gods caused the wine-cup to be miraculously replenished. The knowledge of the language of animals is in both romantic and classical fiction. The ears of Melampus were licked by serpents; and from that time forward he understood the language of birds and other animals. The walking-stick of the priest, which, after he had left the Neck, brought forth leaves and flowers, is like the spear of Romulus, which also put forth leaves in a miraculous manner. The grass grows where the fairies have danced; so also did grass and flowers grow where the classic gods had trodden. The vengeance of Bacchus caused Lycurgus to mutilate himself, in the belief that he was cutting the vines. One of the revelers in Auerbach's cellar in "Faust" is on the point of cutting off his companion's nose, being at the time under the delusion that he is helping himself to a bunch of grapes. The flower which restores the dead to life in the "Lay of Eliduc" has its parallel in classical fiction.

THE SUPERNATURAL IN ROMANTIC FICTION

The Danish folk-tale of the peasant, who transforms himself to a bull, and is sold by his father, is like the story of Erisicthon and Metra, told by Ovid; whilst the annihilation of the Jinnee and of the wizard by the destruction of the bird is not unlike the destruction of Meleager by the burning of the torch. The Greek and Roman deities are sometimes introduced into romance. In the Epic poem of Camoens Venus causes the Portuguese to stay on their return home at an enchanted island, where Thetis and the Nereids entertain them. Venus, since the fall of Paganism, is supposed to reside with other divinities of the same sort in the Venusberg. Diana, or some other heathen goddess, is generally the leader of the witches, when they ride abroad. Mercury, in his various capacities, is often introduced into modern literature, and Apollo, as the literary god, is much mentioned. Centaurs figure as ministers of torture in Dante's poem, and Satyrs are to be found in the "Faerie Queen." In the "Midsummer Night's Dream," Cupid's arrow gives love-producing power to a flower on which it fell; and the flower is used by the fairies. The enchantment, too, of Comus, the son of Circe and Bacchus, is undone by Sabrina. Bacchus, under his name of Sabazius, is supposed to have been the original president at the witches' sabbath. In the "Devil on Two Sticks" Asmodeus asserts himself to be the same as Cupid. Jupiter is introduced into "Cymbeline," but not by Shakespeare. The masque in which this deity appears is undoubtedly an interpolation by an inferior hand. Moliere has, with the aid of Corneille and Quinault, written a spectacular play on the subject of Psyche. Of course, too, in tragedies and other works, founded on classical story, the old gods occasionally make their appearance.

RESEMBLANCES IN FAIRY FICTION

Fairy stories seem to be chiefly derived from the popular traditions of Aryan nations; and it is interesting to observe how remarkably the traditions of various ages and peoples agree. A

THE SUPERNATURAL IN ROMANTIC FICTION

Danish folktale tells how the son of a peasant learns from a
wizard the art of transforming himself into any animal or thing
he pleases. He turns this power to account. He is sold by his
father, in the form of a bull, and then returns in his natural shape
to spend the money. Finally, he has a contest in metamorphoses
with the wizard. After various changes, the peasant boy becomes
a grain of corn. The wizard then becomes a hen in order to eat
the corn; but the boy becomes a hawk, and kills the wizard. In
the story of the second royal mendicant in the "Arabian Nights"
the princess and the Afreet have a similar contest. After many
transformations, the Afreet becomes a pomegranate, which
bursts, and scatters its seeds all round. The princess becomes a
cock, and carefully devours the seeds. One seed, however,
remains undiscovered, and the Afreet has a fresh lease of life. A
story by Straparola is almost identical with the Danish story,
except that in the catastrophe there is more resemblance to the
Arabian story.

In a North German story a wizard keeps a young girl by
force as his wife. He lets out the secret that his soul resides in a
bird, which is locked up in a church in a desert place, and that,
until the bird is killed, he cannot die. The bird is killed by the
girl's lover, and the wizard dies. In the "Arabian Nights" there is
a like story. A Jinnee carries away a princess, and tells her that
his soul resides in a bird, which is shut up in a box, lying at the
bottom of the sea, and that, until the bird is killed, he cannot die.
A prince, possessing a talisman, conjures up the box, kills the
bird, and annihilates the Jinnee. Similar stories are current in
India and Russia. Some of Madame d'Aulnoy's stories are taken
directly from the Italian of Straparola. "Belle Etoile and Prince
Cheri" is so taken. This story is the same as one in the "Arabian
Nights" concerning the two sisters, who were jealous of their
younger sister. Most of Madame d'Aulnoy's stories are founded
on folk-tales. The best and concluding part of the "Blue Bird,"
which resembles a tale in the "Pentamerone," is also like the
conclusion of the Swedish folk-tale "Prince Hatt under the

Earth." Another part of the "Blue Bird," where the transformed prince is nearly cut to pieces by "a razor trap," resembles the Breton "Lay of Ywenec."

"Serpentin Vert" is also like "Prince Hatt." The "Bee and the Orange Tree" resembles in its principal features the Swedish folk-tale of "The Mermaid, the Prince, and the Waiting-maid." There are also similar North German and Russian stories. The "White Cat," besides being similar to the "Frog Bride," the "Enchanted Toad," and "Ahmed and Paribanou," has in other particulars, especially in her disenchantment by decapitation, a marked affinity to Norwegian and North German folktales. "Finette Cendron" is like Cinderella, and the other stories have generally more or less likeness to the popular traditions. The chief incidents of Anthony Hamilton's "Fleur d'Epine" are taken directly, or indirectly, from a Swedish popular story, entitled the "Golden Lantern," and certain other incidents from a Norwegian story, called the "Widow's Son." Hamilton was an Irishman, and possibly there may be some Irish folk-stories akin to these. In Basile's "Pentamerone" an ogre is stopped by magical obstacles very much as Dentue is stopped in "Fleur d'Epine." But there is no horse in the story, and the resemblance is otherwise inexact, whilst the likeness of Hamilton's story to the Northern folk-tales is striking.

"Puss in Boots" is Swedish; and the story has also been told by Straparola, Basile, and Perrault. "Cinderella" is perhaps the most widely known of all stories. The "Sleeping Beauty" is a German folk-story, and was possibly suggested by the legend of the sleeping Brunhild; but it is also in Basile's "Pentamerone," and is likewise to be found in Perrault's collection. A Swedish folk-story tells how a youth was secretly watching a green meadow, when three doves descended, threw aside their plumages, and, becoming three fair maidens, danced on the meadow. The youth got possession of one of the plumages, and would not return it to the damsel to whom it belonged, till she had promised to be his wife. This beautiful story is to be found in many forms. It is the story of the Princess of the Jinn in "Hassan of Balsora," of the sea-maiden, who lost her sealskin; and it somewhat resembles the story of the young man, in the Indian story, whose serpent skin was burnt. Musaeus has written a tale on the same subject. In this tale ladies of fairy origin take the form of swans, and fly to the fountain of youth, in order to bathe therein, and gain perpetual youth and unfading beauty. A young man, instructed of this fact, lay in wait, and saw three swans descend into the rushes that bordered the fountain. Shortly afterwards they came out, and bathed in the water, in the form of beautiful young women. The young man entered the rushes, and saw three veils. He abstracted and secreted one of the veils.

Consequently the young person, to whom it belonged, could not resume her form as a swan, and was compelled to remain behind. One day she recovered her veil, and flew off. In "Dornroschen," or the "Sleeping Beauty," the queen throws a fish, which is on the point of dying, into the water, and the grateful fish promises the fulfillment of her dearest wish, and accomplishes the same. In Madame d'Aulnoy's story of the "Fair One with the Golden Locks" Avenant assists a fish in the same way. He also assists a crow and an owl. In return, the animals promise to reward him, and fulfill their promise. In the "Arabian Nights" a lady helps a serpent, which is equally grateful. In the North German story about the wizard, whose soul resides in a bird, the young man, who is journeying in quest of the bird, behaves kindly on his road to an ox, a boar, and a griffin, and all these creatures assist him in the accomplishment of his adventure. The fables in the "Pleasant Nights" of Straparola are identical with many popular traditions of the North, and tales of the East, either Turkish, Arabian, or Hindu. A story, similar to "Peau d'Ane," has been written by Straparola, but without the supernatural element which exists in the tales of Basile and Perrault.

THE SUPERNATURAL IN ROMANTIC FICTION

"Peau d'Ane" is to be found also in the Russian and Slavonic folk-tales. The first of these stories by Straparola, which deal with the supernatural, is "Prince Piggy," whence Madame d'Aulnoy seems to have derived her "Prince Marcassin." Prince Piggy, who is a pig in the daytime, throws off his pig-skin at night, and becomes a handsome young man. The skin is destroyed, and Prince Piggy acquires permanently a human form. Surely this is the same story as that of the young man whose serpent-skin is burnt. Basile's "Pentamerone," a collection of Neapolitan stories, evidently founded on folk-tales, appeared in the earlier part of the seventeenth century, about a hundred years after the publication of Straparola's work. There are many stones in Basile similar to those in Straparola, though differing from them so much as to show that they are not imitations. Stories, like "Peau d'Ane" and "Puss in Boots" are in Basile; also the universal "Cinderella"; also a story resembling "Prince Hatt," and another, resembling the "Sleeping Beauty."

The young man whose serpent skin was burnt is also to be found there. Thorpe's "Yule Tide Stories" and Ralston's "Russian Folk Tales" are two modern works, from which much information may be gained concerning folk-stories.

MIGRATION OF SOULS

The possibility of a person's identity migrating into another body during life is the subject of several imaginative tales; among others of a Persian tale, of which the following is the substance. Fadlallah, king of Mousel and husband of Zemroude, became very friendly with a young dervish. Whilst the two were hunting, the dervish told the king that he had learned from a Brahmin the secret of reanimating a dead body, by causing his own soul to pass into it. To prove this, he tried the experiment on a doe, which the king had killed. The body of the dervish fell lifeless, and the doe was reanimated. The soul, then, re-entered the body of the dervish. At the request of the king, the dervish communicated the secret to him. The king, then, in his turn caused his own soul to enter the body of the doe. As soon, however, as he had done so, the dervish caused his own soul to enter the body of the king, and tried to shoot the transformed Fadlallah, who escaped into the woods.

The dervish then returned to Mousel, and filled the throne and bed of Fadlallah. It will be remembered that in the same way the soul of the Stranger passes into the body of Arnold in Lord Byron's "Deformed Transformed." An union of three souls in one body is to be found in Spenser's "Faerie Queen." When Priamond and Diamond are slain, their souls take up their abode in the body of their surviving brother, Triamond.

DEATH

Death is generally personified as a skeleton. Milton's conception of it is more imposing. He describes it as shapeless, unsubstantial, shaking a dreadful dart, and having the likeness of a kingly crown on what seemed its head. Death is a personage in Fouques' "Sintram," which is rather a weak romance, having been written for the purpose of illustrating a picture. In the "Castle of Otranto" a skeleton appears in the garb of a monk; but this is rather the apparition of a dead man than the image of Death itself. In a drama by Calderon on the "Purgatory of Patrick," a figure uncloaks itself, and reveals to Lodovico Enio the form of a skeleton. In Slavonic folk-tales the plague is personified as a woman of hideous aspect. That the wounds of a murdered man should bleed afresh, whenever the murderer approaches the corpse, is a common superstition. In the "Nibelungen Lied," the body of Siegfried thus proves the guilt of Gunther. Southey has a ballad, founded on one of the lays of Marie de France, on the subject of Sir Owen's descent into Purgatory. Sir Owen himself is alive, but he sees the place where the dead are. He gets very much frozen and very much burnt; and finally awakes to life at the entrance of the cavern into which he had descended.

The aborigines of Mexico believed that the souls of the good became clouds or beautiful birds, or precious stones, and that the souls of the bad become beetles, rats, and other vile animals. The souls of defunct Mussulmans are supposed to inhabit green birds. Lord Byron, in the "Bride of Abydos," passes the soul of Selim into a bulbul, and that of Zuleika into a rose. The following story may perhaps here find its right place. A Spanish cavalier was in the habit of visiting a nun, with whom he had an intrigue. One night, on his way to her, he passed a church, where burial service was being performed for the dead. He asked the priest for the name of the dead person. To his horror and dismay, they mentioned his own name. He mounted his horse, and returned home, but was accompanied by two strange dogs. Immediately that he dismounted at his house, the dogs strangled him. As the circumstances could only be divulged by himself, it is not apparent how they were made known. The story is told by Alexandre Dumas, and is also mentioned by the Abbe Bordelon, in the "Adventures of Monsieur Oufle," as coming from the "Hexameron."

VAMPIRES, AND ANIMATED CORPSES

When a vampire dies, he rises from his grave at night, and supports a fresh existence by sucking the blood of other persons whilst they are asleep.

These other persons soon die, and themselves become vampires. A body suspected of Vampirism is disinterred, and is generally recognized by the freshness of the face. A stake is driven through the heart of the vampire, who then utters a loud scream. The body is burnt to ashes. This is supposed to be the only way of finally getting rid of the nuisance. Lord Byron's lines in the "Giaour" will be remembered. A story is to be found in Phlegon's treatise on wonderful things concerning a girl of the name of Philinnium, a native of Tralles, in Asia Minor, who not only after her death visited her lover, but ate, drank, and even cohabited with him. This event, which happened in the time of the Emperor Hadrian, is the subject of Goethe's poem, "The Bride of Corinth." Similar stories have been told by Alexandre Dumas, Washington Irving, and perhaps by others. Hauff has a story concerning a vessel, which a couple of shipwrecked sailors boarded. They found only corpses in the vessel, but at nighttime these corpses were animated, and worked the ship. In Coleridge's "Ancient Mariner" dead seamen are reanimated. In a story by Marryat, half the crew of a vessel murdered the other half, including the boatswain, and threw their bodies overboard. At night the guilty survivors hear the boatswain's whistle, accompanied by the summons for all hands to go on deck. They go, and find the corpses, of which they thought they had rid themselves, still on deck. They try to throw them into the sea again, but the corpses cling to the murderers, and roll with them overboard.

GHOSTS

Apparitions are generally ghosts, but there may be apparitions, raised by magic or witchcraft, which are not ghosts. Such are the apparitions of the armed head, bloody child, and eight kings in "Macbeth." The apparitions of the dead have always been an important element in the supernatural. Among others, the spirit of Caligula is said to have walked very much in the manner of a modern ghost. It will be quite impossible to deal completely with the ghosts that belong to romantic fiction. Some, like the spirits of Hamlet a Guido Cavalcanti, are too celebrated to require mention; others are too numerous and too insignificant.

A few, however, will be specified. The Wild Huntsman, if not himself a ghost, is always in ghostly company. He is supposed by some to be Odin, by others to be one of the classic gods. He issues from the Venusberg, the refuge of the classic gods of antiquity, who fled thither on the prevalence of Christianity. He rides on stormy nights, followed by a train both of the living and the dead. The ghost of the Trusty Eckart, who died contending with the demons of the Venusberg, and who in vain warned Tannenhauser not to enter it, precedes the hellish crew, and warns men of their approach. For it is dangerous to meet them; and if any person is so unfortunate as to come across them, he is generally smitten with paralysis or insanity. Those who have met nymphs, peris, and fairies seem to have been liable to a similar mischief. Herne the Hunter, described by Shakespeare, is a ghost who bears some resemblance to the Wild Huntsman. The Willis, or Wilis (for the name seems to be spelled either way), exist chiefly in Hungary. They are the spirits of brides, who die on their wedding-day before consummation of marriage. They are to be seen by moonlight, where cross-roads meet; and they dance to death any unlucky man who encounters them. The story of Burger's "Lenore" is this: Lenore's lover, William, had fought on King Frederick's side at the battle of Prague. The army returns, but no news is heard of William; and Lenore, in spite of her mother's supplications, curses God. At midnight she hears the tramp of a horse's hoofs beneath the window, and the voice of her lover calling her to ride with him to their wedding-bed. She descends and mounts behind him, learning too late that she is carried off by the specter of her lover, who is bearing her to the grave, to punish her for her blasphemy. This, however, may perhaps be more properly considered a devil in the form of a lover than a ghost.

Another German ghost is the Bleeding Nun. This was a nun who, after committing many crimes and debaucheries, was assassinated by one of her paramours, and denied the rites of burial. After this she used to haunt the castle, where she was murdered, in her nun's dress, with her bleeding wounds. On one occasion, a young lady of the castle, wishing to elope with her lover, in order to make her flight easier, impersonated the bleeding nun. Unfortunately the lover, whilst expecting his lady under this disguise, eloped with the specter herself, who presented herself to him and haunted him afterwards. This story is told by Lewis in his "Monk," and also by Musaeus. The Belludo is a Spanish ghost, mentioned by Washington Irving in his "Tales of the Alhambra." It issues forth in the dead of night, and scours the avenues of the Alhambra and the streets of Granada, in the shape of a headless horse, pursued by six hounds, with terrible yells and howlings. It is said to be the spirit of a Moorish king, who killed his six sons. And these sons hunt him in the shape of hounds at night-time in revenge. Besides the apparitions of the dead, there are apparitions of the living.

It is mentioned, in one of the notes to "Monsieur Oufle," by the Abbe Bordelon, that monks and nuns, a short time before their death, have seen the images of themselves seated in their chairs or stalls. Another example may be given. Catherine of Russia, after retiring to her bedroom, was told that she had been seen just before to enter the state chamber. On hearing this she went thither, and saw the exact similitude of herself seated upon the throne. She ordered her guards to fire upon it.

Another sort of ghost of the living is mentioned in an Eastern story. A soldier of the guard of a certain king met a spirit in the form of a beautiful woman, who was wailing bitterly; and she told him that she was the soul of the king, his master, who was fated to die within three days. Ghosts sometimes leave behind them substantial marks of their visits. In Scott's well-known ballad the phantom knight impresses an indelible mark on the lady who has been his paramour. In the Tartar stories, written by a Frenchman, a series of stories neither original nor well constructed, a ghost appears to Prince Faruk in a dream, and touches him on the arm. The prince finds the mark of the burn when he awakes.

THE SUPERNATURAL IN ROMANTIC FICTION

SEA PHANTOMS

Davy Jones, mentioned often enough by Smollett, Marryat, and others, is the name of a devil, who is hostile to sailors when at sea, and occasionally makes himself visible to them. A similar apparition, Adamastor, the giant spirit of the Cape, is to be found in the "Lusiads" of Camoens. The Flying Dutchman is the phantom vessel whose appearance foretells woe to those who see it. The fire of Saint Hermes is a supernatural fire, which betokens bad weather, and shows itself in various parts of a ship. Ariel converted himself into this fire, and describes it:

> I boarded the king's ship; now on the beak,
> Now in the waist, the deck, in every cabin
> I flamed amazement; sometimes I'd divide,
> And burn in many places; on the top-mast,
> The yards and bow-sprit, would I flame distinctly,
> Then meet and join.

Saint Hermes is also called Saint Hermo and Saint Elmo. Dryden, in one of his songs, speaks of "Saint Hermo, that sits upon the sails." Sir Walter Scott, in his note on this passage, says that the fire of Saint Hermo foretold good weather. This seems to be a mistake.

HAUNTED HOUSES

Ali of Cairo, in the "Arabian Nights," was taken to a deserted house, but was advised not to lodge there, being told that the house was haunted, and that every one who had passed the night in it had become a corpse before morning. Ali, being in a desperate condition, determined to pass the night in the house, thinking that to do so would be a very convenient way of committing suicide. He supped in a magnificent saloon of the house, and was about to retire to bed, when a voice said: "Ali, shall I send thee down gold?"

Thereupon a shower of gold fell into the apartment. It was a Jinnee that haunted the place. Ali was the person for whom the gold was destined. The Jinnee had killed all the wrong persons who had lodged in the house, and now benefited the right person. Stories of haunted houses are very common in the literature of modern Europe. For instance, the apparition of a bleeding child always presented itself to anybody, staying in a particular house, who was destined to die a violent death. In another house the sound of some one, drumming through all the passages, was always heard just before the death of any of the family to whom the house belonged. The child and the drummer had originally been murdered in these houses; and their ghosts in consequence made themselves disagreeable. In Scott's "Tapestried Chamber," the ghost that haunts the chamber is an old woman. It may be seen in the "Mostellaria" of Plautus that haunted houses were not unknown to the Greeks and Romans.

PROGNOSTICS

The "Macbeth" of Shakespeare and the "Bard" of Gray are splendid examples of the important place that a foreknowledge of events takes in romantic fiction. Innumerable other instances might be given; but, perhaps, the following from the "Tales of the Alhambra" is as good as any. A Moorish king of Granada had a son, named Ahmed. At the birth of this son, the astrologers predicted that he would suffer great danger, unless he were kept from the knowledge of love during his early youth. He was accordingly immured in a high tower, and apparently separated from the possibility of acquiring the dangerous knowledge. But of course these precautions were unavailing. Disembodied spirits have a privilege of prognostication. Thus Fergus Mac Ivor, in "Waverley," is warned of approaching death by the family ghost. The living body is supposed sometimes to

THE SUPERNATURAL IN ROMANTIC FICTION

prognosticate. The witch in "Macbeth" says:

> By the pricking of my thumbs
> Something wicked this way comes.

The Banshee, who is a fairy with the manners of a ghost, is in the habit of wailing at windows before the death of any person in whom she feels an interest. The approaching death of a person is sometimes announced by the appearance of supernatural lights. Thus, in the song in the "Lay of the Last Minstrel" it is narrated that before the death of lovely Rosabelle a blaze of supernatural fire was seen. Living people have the gift of second sight. For instance, a person sees a phantom funeral. Shortly afterwards a death occurs, and he sees the real funeral, similar, in all respects, to what he had previously seen. There is a fable, which looks rather spurious, but is included with the other fables of Aesop, and it is as follows. It was prophesied that the son of a man should be killed by a lion. Thereupon the father shut his son up in a tower. But there was a picture of a lion in the tower; and the young man scratched himself with a nail in the picture. Gangrene and death ensued, so it came to pass, after all, that the young man was killed by a lion. The above is one of many stories illustrating the inevitable verification of a prediction, notwithstanding preventive measures. Prognostics may be in the form of curses, as in the "Gesta Romanorum," where a marvelous stag prophesied that its pursuer should kill his parents; and the prophecy was accomplished. The actions of birds do not furnish prognostics so much as they used to do in ancient times. Yet the death of Duncan was foreshadowed by the slaughter of the falcon by the mousing-owl.

SUPERNATURAL DREAMS AND VISIONS

The commonest form of a supernatural dream is this. Two intimate friends make a compact that, if one dies, he will somehow communicate the fact to the other. Shortly afterwards one of them starts on his travels. The other then dreams that his friend appears to him with his throat cut, and tells him that he has been murdered, and also informs him where his body may be found. This dream is repeated night after night; whereupon the surviving friend acts according to the instructions he has received in the dream, discovers the corpse, and convicts the murderer. The above, with variations, is the subject of many stories, the oldest of which is classical. Fouque has written a story called "Aslauga's Knight." The hero of it, Froda, reads in a chronicle concerning Siegfried's daughter, Aslauga, who has been dead a hundred years. He vows to be her faithful knight, notwithstanding her decease. In return, she constantly appears to him in a vision. At last he dies, happy in the thought that he is about to be united to her. Somewhat in the same manner does Shelley's Alastor live and die in the search of a phantom mistress, who occasionally appears to him. There is a Chinese story of a certain Liyi, who was murdered by Wang-kia.

The murderer is tried for the crime, but acquitted. As he is escorted to his home in triumph by his friends, a cold gust of wind comes upon the party. The murderer cries, "I am lost! I see Liyi; he throws himself upon me!" And with these words he falls, and expires. The well-known drama of the "Corsican Brothers" is founded on a story which Alexandre Dumas relates as being within his own personal experiences. Louis and Lucien de Franchi are twin brothers. They come of a family which have the supernatural habit of revealing themselves, one to another, at the hour of death.

Louis is killed at Paris by Monsieur de Chateau-Renard. At the moment of his death he appears to his brother in Corsica, and, in a vision, acquaints him with the circumstances of the duel. Lucien then goes to Paris, and kills Chateau-Renard. In some dreams the presence seems to be divided. A person is transported to another place, leaving his sleeping body behind. In the "Ingoldsby Legends" there is a story, in which, by means of magic, iniquities, of which she is conscious, are perpetrated upon a sleeping girl; she being asleep in one place, whilst her persecutors are in another place. In "Undine" Huldbrand falls asleep, and is borne by swans to the Mediterranean, where he hears a conversation between Undine and Kuhleborn, although his body still remains where he fell asleep. In Dryden's fable of "The Cock and the Fox" there is a summary of supernatural dreams.

CURSES AND BLESSINGS

The supernatural effect of a curse may be produced in various ways. The mother of Robert the Devil devoted her son to the arch-enemy, who took possession of the child, and inspired him with his own wickedness. Roderick gave effect to the curse on Spain by entering the enchanted tower of Toledo. The little jack-daw, which stole the cardinal's ring, was cursed formally. A story in Marryat's "Phantom Ship" tells how a hunter in the Harz mountains marries a werewolf. He kills her, on detecting her in the act of devouring the flesh of his dead child, whereupon her body, which was that of a comely young woman, changes into its original form of a white wolf. The hunter, when he married her, had sworn by the spirits of the Harz mountains never to harm his wife, and had invoked upon himself and his children the curse, if he did so, of being torn to pieces by wild beasts. The curse is fulfilled. The following will do as an example of Blessings. In a Turkish story a tailor finds a purse, and gives it to the rightful owner, a coja, or doctor. The coja, instead of sharing the purse with the finder, rewards him cheaply, as he imagines, with a silent prayer in his behalf. Quite, however, against his inclination, he is compelled by some secret power to offer up the following prayer: "O Allah! Let all that is mine become one day the property of this young man!" This involuntary blessing is realized. The wife of the coja and all his property finally belong to the tailor.

THE SUPERNATURAL IN ROMANTIC FICTION

THE EVIL EYE

In one of the "Persian Tales" there is a princess so dangerously beautiful, that any young man who meets her eye immediately becomes mad. The Caliph Vathek had the gift of the evil eye. Whenever he was angry, his look would slay the person who had offended him. Alexandre Dumas tells a story of a Neapolitan prince, who was the best meaning person possible, but had unfortunately an evil eye, the power of which he exercised quite unconsciously. He went to a ball, and, having caused all sorts of accidents by simply looking at persons and things, he took leave of his irate hostess, assuring her that he had never spent so charming an evening. He went on board ship, and caused a storm, which wrecked the vessel, by simply looking to see how the weather was. When his daughter married, he looked at her husband, and pronounced a benediction on the wedded pair. The consequence was a divorce.

A Slavonic folk story tells how the evil eye exercised its influence after death, when it was dug up from the ground in which it had been buried. The Basilisk, or Cockatrice, may be taken as an example of an animal possessing an evil eye.

DEVILS

The seven arch-fiends appear to be Beelzebub, Belial, Asmodeus, Satan or Lucifer, Mephistopheles, Abaddon or Apollyon, and Mammon. Satan is generally, but not always, considered the prince of them all. He is so considered in Milton's great poem, in which most of the other above-mentioned devils are also conspicuous. Beelzebub is the devil of Cazotte's "Diable Amoureux." Asmodeus is the devil on two sticks of Le Sage's novel. Mephistopheles is the evil genius of Goethe's "Faust" Apollyon is the antagonist of Christian in Bunyan's "Pilgrim's Progress." Mammon is the tempter of Sir Guyon in Spenser's

"Faerie Queen." Zamiel, though not so great as the above, was a devil of distinction. He was the paramour of Lilith. He is also known as the evil spirit in "Der Freischutz."

Naturally the chief occupation of these infernal spirits is the capture, by fair means or foul, of human beings. Faust deliberately sold himself to the Evil One. Don Juan lost himself through his bad deeds, without entering into any special contract. Der Freischutz sold himself for seven enchanted bullets, of which the seventh went as the devil listed. Peter Schlemihl sold his shadow, as well as himself, for the purse of Fortunatus, and then, putting on the seven-league boots, diverted his mind from unpleasant thoughts by running about the world. Robert the Devil was devoted to the enemy of mankind by his mother at the moment of conception; and there is in the "Gesta Romanorum" a story of a girl heedlessly devoted to the devil, and carried off accordingly. Burton in his "Anatomy of Melancholy" and Wierus say that, at Hammel, in Saxony, the devil, in the likeness of a pied piper, carried away one hundred and thirty children. Wierus tells how Pope Benedict the Ninth was strangled by a devil in a forest, and, after death, appeared in the likeness of a bear with an ass's head. The "Monk" of Lewis treats of temptation by a devil, and is apparently founded on a Turkish story. The tale, told by Straparola and others, concerning the devil, who went back to his infernal abode, in order to escape from a woman, bears also a strong resemblance to a Turkish story. Belphegor is the name of this devil, according to Boccaccio, who is one of the tellers of the story. The story is not in the "Decameron," but in another of his works.

Hoffmann has written a novel on the subject of the Devil's Elixir, the property of which was of course to tempt to evil. According to this tale, when St. Anthony was in the desert, he obtained a bottle of this elixir from the devil, and deposited it in a certain monastery. After many centuries, Brother Medardus, the custodian of the elixir, drinks it, and, fired with new desires, quits the cloister. He commits many crimes under the influence of the liquor, but is finally saved. Of the devils in the Arabian Mythology, Eblis, formerly called Azazeel, is chief. He will be best described in a passage from Beckford's admirable "Vathek."

The formidable Eblis was seated upon a globe of fire. His figure was that of a young man of twenty years of age, the noble and regular features of whom seemed to have been blasted by malignant vapors. Despair and pride were painted in his great eyes; and his waving hair yet resembled a little that of an angel of light. In his hand, delicate but blackened by lightning, he held the brazen scepter, which makes tremble all the powers of the abyss. The Incubi and Succubi are devils, of whom the incubi are in the shape of men, the succubi in the shape of women. Lilith may be considered a succubus, for she was a devil who was united to Adam, and bore him a supernatural progeny. Of late, however, she has borne the character of a witch. In Middleton's play of the "Witch" Hecate speaks of a custom that witches have, of causing their familiar spirits to assume the form of any man for whom they may have a passion. These spirits are ordinarily in the form of a cat. It has been observed that witches have a spirit in this form because Diana, or Hecate, the ancient goddess of witchcraft, was once transformed to a cat.

The night-mare is supposed to be a demon that oppresses people in their sleep. Hecate, in the above-mentioned play, says: "The Night-mare shall call thee when she walks." According to Edgar's song in "Lear" the night-mare was exorcised by St. Withold. The following is mentioned as an anecdote of a succubus in Burton's "Anatomy of Melancholy." A young gentleman of Rome, the day he was married, put a ring upon the finger of a statue of Venus, whilst he was playing tennis. On going to resume his ring, he found that the hand of the statue had closed, and that he could not recover the ring. At night-time the likeness of Venus came between him and his wife, prevented him from consummating his marriage, and continued to do so until the devil was laid. Cazotte's "Diable Amoureux" may be here considered. In that work a young Spanish gentleman, named Alvarez, is the speaker throughout the story, and relates the adventure as happening to himself. He is a captain in the guards of the King of Naples; and, among his brother officers is one, named Soberano, who is a cabalist, or, in other words, skilled in the science of transmuting metals, and enslaving the elementary spirits. Alvarez burns with desire to communicate with the spirits, and presses Soberano to give him at once the means of doing so. Soberano intimates that, to accomplish his desire without danger to himself, he should first pass through some long term of probation. But the impatience of Alvarez will not permit him to do this. He declares that nothing, however terrible, can shake his resolution, and that he would pull the ears of the biggest devil in hell.

Seeing him thus resolved, Soberano let him have his way. They dine together, in company with two friends of Soberano, who are also cabalists, and then set out to the ruins of Portici. Proceeding through the ruins, they arrive at a vault, in which Soberano inscribes a magic circle. He instructs Alvarez to enter the circle, and pronounce certain words, calling out three times the name of Beelzebub. He, then, with his companions, withdraws. Alvarez, left to himself, pronounces the words, and calls on the devil, according to his instructions. Hardly has he done so, when a window opens, opposite to him, at the top of the vault; a torrent of light, more dazzling than that of day, bursts through the opening : the head of a camel, huge and horrible, with ears of enormous size, shows itself at the window, and cries out: Che vuoi?

Alvarez sustains his courage, and orders the phantom to appear under another form. Thereupon the camel vomits a white spaniel, with ears sweeping the ground, and vanishes. As Alvarez makes a movement to pull the spaniel's ears, it throws itself on its back, and he perceives that it is a female. The dog, or rather bitch, afterwards appears in the form of a beautiful woman, to whom Alvarez gives the name of Biondetta. She, submissive, and to all appearance passionately attached to her master, does all in her power to form with him the closest connection. Alvarez, although by no means insensible to her fascinations, is somewhat alarmed at the prospect of thus giving himself utterly to the devil. She, however, explains to him that she was not the camel that appeared to him in the first instance; but that she is a sylphide, who, having fallen in love with him, and assumed the form of a woman, is now doomed to continue such. As a compromise, he proposes marriage, but she naturally shrinks from anything so proper, and redoubles her efforts to seduce him.

At last she is successful, and then the following conversation and scene take place. With a voice, to whose sweetness no music could be compared, she said: "Have I made the happiness of my Alvarez as he has made mine? But no; I am still the only happy one; he shall be so; I will intoxicate him with pleasure; I will fill him with knowledge; I will raise him to the summit of greatness. Wilt thou, beloved, be the most privileged of creatures, and rule with me over mankind, over the elements, over all nature?"

"Oh, dear Biondetta," I said, "thou art sufficient for me; thou fulfillest all the desires of my heart."

"No! No!" she said quickly, "Biondetta is not sufficient for thee; that is not my name; it flattered me; I bore it with pleasure; but it is necessary that thou shouldst know who I am. I am the devil, my dear Alvarez, I am the devil." She pronounced this word with an accent of enchanting sweetness.

"Cease," I said, "my dear Biondetta, or whosoever thou mayst be, to pronounce that fatal name, and recall to me a mistake long since abjured."

"No, my dear Alvarez, no, it was not a mistake; I was obliged to make thee believe so, my pet. It was necessary to deceive thee in order to make thee reasonable. Thou seest I am not so black as I am represented to be." This badinage disconcerted me. "But answer then," she said. "And what shall I answer?"

"Ingrate, place thy hand on the heart adores thee; let a little of the delicious fire that burns in my veins be infused into thine; soften, if thou canst, the sound of that voice, so fit to inspire love, which thou usest only to terrify my timid soul; say to me, but with all the tenderness that I feel for thee, 'My dear Beelzebub, I adore thee.'"

At this fatal name, though so tenderly pronounced, a mortal terror seized me; stupor and astonishment crushed my soul. She did not give me time to recover myself, and reflect on my folly. Without perceptibly altering the tone of her voice, she continued:

"Thou earnest to seek me; I have followed thee, served thee, assisted thee, and have fulfilled all thy wishes. I desired possession of thee, and, in order that I should obtain it, it was necessary that thou shouldst abandon thyself freely to me. Henceforth, Alvarez, our union is indissoluble, but it is important for us to know each other. As I already know thee by heart, in order to make the advantage reciprocal, I must show myself to thee as I really am."

I had no time to reflect on this singular harangue. I heard a sharp hissing at my side... I turned my eyes. Instead of the ravishing figure, what did I see? Oh! Heaven! it was the frightful head of the camel. It articulated with a voice of thunder the gloomy Che vuoi? which had so terrified me before, burst into a fit of human laughter more dreadful still, and put out a monstrous tongue.

THE SUPERNATURAL IN ROMANTIC FICTION

In Marlowe's tragedy of "Doctor Faustus" a devil takes the form of Helen of Troy. It may indeed have been the spirit of the real Helen that was summoned for the occasion; but it is more likely that it was a succubus. Temptation by a devil in the form of a woman is very common in literature. There is an instance of it in Dryden's "King Arthur." A legend, on which Walter Scott has founded a ballad, tells how two hunters met two beautiful ladies in green. One of the hunters goes off with one of the green ladies. The other is more prudent. After a time he goes in quest of his companion, and discovers that he has been torn to pieces by the devil, that had assumed so fascinating a form.

DIVINE POWER IN ROMANCE

The following story is told of Azrae'l, the angel of death. He once passed by Solomon in a visible shape, and looked at a man that was sitting by the king. The man asked concerning him, and upon Solomon telling him that it was the angel of death, he said: "He seems to want me; wherefore order the wind to carry me from here to India."

This being done, the angel said to Solomon: "I looked so earnestly at the man out of wonder, because I was commanded to take his soul in India, and found him with thee in Palestine."

Harut and Marut, two celebrated angels in the Arabian Mythology, expressed contempt for Man because he was fallen, and were sent down themselves on earth to be tried. They were tempted by Zohara, or the planet Venus, in the shape of a beautiful woman. They yielded, and are punished by divine wrath until the day of judgment. They are hung up by the feet with their heads downwards, between heaven and earth, in the territory of Babel. They can be heard, but not seen. There is a legend that the cross, whereon Christ was crucified, was made from a tree, which was sown by Adam, and miraculously preserved for the occasion. The cross is also said to have been made of the wood of the aspen tree; and, ever since the crucifixion, the leaves of this tree have trembled in commemoration of the dire event. The legend of "Placidus" relates how a crucifix appeared between the horns of a hunted stag, and spoke. The story of the Wandering Jew is that he insulted Jesus at the crucifixion, and, for this act was doomed to wander on earth until the day of judgment. In "La Mort d'Arthur" the knight Balen enters the castle of King Pelles. In a fight with the king he breaks his sword, and, hotly pursued by Pelles, he flees from room to room, until he enters a chamber, where he finds a spear. He seizes this, and with it runs the king through the body. Immediately that he does so, a violent thunderstorm breaks forth, and the castle tumbles to the ground. Balen is stunned at first, but, recovering, finds himself lying among the ruins, and perceives the enchanter Merlin, standing near, who informs him that the spear was the same that spilled the blood of Christ, and that from the dolorous stroke which had been given much mischief had arisen, and would yet arise. Some time after the death of Christ, but before the birth of Mahomet, Abu Navass was ruler in the land of Yemen. He himself was a fire-worshiper, but his own son had become a Christian. Furious with his son for the bad example he was setting to the people, Abu Navass ordered him to be put to death. But, although thrown into the sea, into a fiery furnace, and shot at with arrows, he was each time miraculously preserved, and said to his father: "Own now that my God is the true God.", "Only tell me the secret how to slay thee," was the answer of the angry father. "Aim an arrow at my heart in the name of my God," said the son. "Then die in the name of thy God," said the father. As he spoke, he shot the arrow and killed his son. A German legend tells how a drunken knight rode up to the altar of a church. The earth opened, and horse and rider sank into the abyss. The four horseshoes, however, remained behind, and were nailed to the church door as a memorial of the miracle.

The supernatural story of the Wildgrave, who was

punished for hunting on Sunday, has been told by Burger. There is a legend which tells how Bishop Hatto was, on account of his wickedness, devoured by an army of rats or mice, sent especially for this purpose by divine power. A collection of Turkish stories, of which use has already been made in this work, were translated into French not much later than the time of the introduction of the "Arabian Nights" and "Persian Tales" to the notice of the West. They are supposed to be told by the viziers of a sultan of Persia to their master on the one hand, and by the sultana to him on the other hand. The stories of the viziers, being told for the purpose of defeating the plans of the sultana, all harp upon the perfidy and wickedness of women, but unconsciously they exhibit even more conspicuously the cruelty and selfishness of men.

The sultana has to hold her own against all this ministerial wisdom. Never was there so vacillating a monarch as her husband. He changes his mind with the hearing of every story, and oscillates in his purpose with the regularity of a pendulum. In one story the sultana tells him how the Jews once deserted Moses, in spite of the remonstrances of the women; and she winds up her narrative by saying that he is quite as weak as the Jews. The divine power that is exhibited in the tale is this. The king of Ad and his people are giants, and, when Moses goes alone to meet them, the king throws a rock at the prophet. An angel, however, in the shape of a bird, descends, splits the rock with his beak, and causes the fragments to pass harmlessly on either side of Moses. Then, by divine power, Moses increases in bulk till he equals the king, whom he kills, when the people of Ad take to flight. In the story of the first royal mendicant in the "Arabian Nights," the wrath of heaven is displayed, and an impious prince is burnt to ashes by lightning, especially sent for his destruction. King Antiochus had a similar fate.

In the lady's story in the "Arabian Nights," celestial wrath changes an idolatrous people into stone. As an example of divine power one may notice the overthrow of Satan and his horrid crew in "Paradise Lost," and their subsequent transformation to serpents. A story is told in the "Spectator" of divine chastisement for the involuntary neglect of the sacred duty of ablution. A dervish of great sanctity one morning broke a crystal cup which was consecrated to the prophet. A short time after, the son of the dervish came, in order to receive as usual the paternal blessing. His father blessed him, but, immediately after, the young man fell and broke his arm. Whilst the old man was grieving over this last misfortune, a caravan from Mecca passed by. He went up to one of the holy camels, and stroked it; whereupon the animal kicked him and hurt him very much. He then remembered that he had forgotten to wash his hands that morning. An indelible blood-stain, consequent upon murder, is a common effect of divine wrath in romance. In the story of "Alexius," and elsewhere, divine power is shown by a mysterious voice.

VALKYRS

The Valkyrs are demi-goddesses in the Scandinavian Mythology. They are the only females admitted into Odin's paradise, the Valhalla. They are the messengers of the gods, and ride through the air on shadowy horses, and sometimes take the form of wild swans. They weave the web of the fate of warriors, as may be learned from Gray's translation, "The Fatal Sisters." Of the Valkyrs Brunhild is perhaps the most celebrated. Sigurd, who learned the language of birds by eating the heart of a serpent, discovered Brunhild asleep in full armor. He pulled off the armor, and she awoke from an enchanted sleep, into which she had been cast by Odin. Sigurd avowed his love for her, but she, who knew the future, told him that he would be the husband of another. Sigurd married Gudrun, and played Brunhild a very scurvy trick, similar to that which Siegfried played Brunhild in the "Nibelungen Lied." Brunhild revenged herself upon him by killing him; and then showed her love for him by killing herself.

THE SUPERNATURAL IN ROMANTIC FICTION

Sigurd and Brunhild were united in Paradise. The "Nibelungen Lied" is founded on this legend.

The story of Volund and the Valkyrs has some similarity to that in "Hassan of Balsora," already mentioned, and to other legends of the same sort.

SCANDINAVIAN DEITIES

The celestial city, the abode of these gods, situated in the center of the universe, was called Asgard; and the rainbow was the bridge which led to it. Odin was the chief Scandinavian deity. He was made acquainted with everything, that happened on earth, through the agency of two ravens, representing Observation and Memory. He was the husband of Freya, or Frigga, and father of Thor and Balder. The Valhalla was his palace, where were received the souls of warriors killed in battle. On having a presentiment that Balder was to die, he descended into the infernal regions, to consult Hela. This descent forms the subject of an exquisite translation by Gray. Loki, though among the gods, was a traitor to them. He was the father of two monsters, that are to be the chief instruments in the destruction of the world. These monsters are the wolf Fenrir, and the serpent Jormangundur, which lies at the bottom of the ocean, and encompasses the world. The wolf Fenrir was bound, but not before he had bitten off the hand of Tyr, one of the gods. At Ragnarok, the twilight of the gods, the wolf Fenrir will get loose, and assist in the universal destruction. It was through Loki that Balder was slain. Freya, having a presentiment that Balder was to die, made everything animate and inanimate, except the mistletoe, which was forgotten, swear to do him no harm. Loki made a spear of mistletoe, and put it into the hand of Hodur, the blind god, and brother of Balder. Hodur unintentionally slew Balder with this spear. Thereupon the gods bound Loki, and very cruelly put him to unceasing torture. Of Thor, the most celebrated, after Odin, of the Scandinavian gods, the following legend is related. On one occasion he paid a visit to Utgardelok, king of the giants, and failed to achieve three apparently easy feats.

He was challenged first to drink a horn dry, but, with all his efforts, could not diminish the liquor in it. He then tried unsuccessfully to lift a cat; and finally wrestled with an old woman, who worsted him. It was, however, afterwards explained to him that the feats he had attempted were much greater than they appeared; for that in drinking from the horn, he had been trying to drink the sea; that the cat was the great serpent, Jormangundur; and that the old woman was Time.

HINDU DEITIES

Brahma, the creator, Vishnu, the preserver, and Siva, or Mahadeo, the destroyer, constitute the Trimurti, or Hindu Trinity. They, however, are not immortal. They will die with the other gods in the end; and nothing and nobody will survive, except Brahma the eternal. Once upon a time Brahma and Vishnu contended for supremacy in the universe. Siva came between them in the shape of a column of fire, and, acting as arbitrator, said that he should be considered supreme god, who could find the end of the column. Vishnu, thereupon, started to find one end, whilst Brahma sought to find the other end. After going at the rate of something like a thousand miles a second for a thousand years, it suddenly occurred to Vishnu that the column was infinite. He thereupon frankly acknowledged the supremacy of Siva, who is certainly not a finite being in this legend. Brahma was not so honest. He pretended to have found the end of the column. From that time Siva and Vishnu have been good friends, but they have been estranged from Brahma. Siva is the principle of fire. Siva's wife once playfully put her hands over his eyes only for an instant; but an instant with gods is an age with men; and the result of the goddess's little joke was that the universe remained without light for an incalculable time. Camdeo, the god of love, attempted to wound Siva, but was reduced to ashes by that superior god, and since that time only survives as an essence. Goethe has written a beautiful poem, "The God and the Bayadere," upon a supposed avatar of Mahadeo. Vishnu, however, is the god who is celebrated for his avatars or incarnations. He has had nine of them; and the tenth is yet to come. His most famous avatars are those of Rama, Krishna, and Buddha. Rama once mutilated a monster by cutting off its arms, if not its head. The monster, which was an enchanted being, thereupon recovered its pristine beauty, and thanked the god for the apparently cruel but really beneficial act. Hanuman is the monkey-god, who in combat with a monster enlarged and reduced himself at will. Rama and his army were once rendered insensible by magical weapons. The effects of the magic were only to be removed by the application of a certain plant. Hanuman went to seek it. The plant grew on a mountain, and Hanuman was instructed that this plant would be illuminated by a lamp placed under it. When Hanuman arrived at the mountain he found that Indra, in order to perplex him, had placed a lamp under every plant that grew on the mountain. Hanuman, however, was equal to the occasion. He carried away the mountain, with everything that grew on it. Most of the above may be found in Moor's "Hindu Pantheon."

HEROES OF ROMANCE

"La Mort d'Arthur" relates the adventures of Arthur, king of Britain, and of the Knights of the Round Table. In that book it is told how an arm appeared above the lake, holding the sword Excalibur, which Arthur took, and how when he was wounded to death, Sir Bedivere, acting by his instructions, flung the sword back into the lake, when the arm reappeared, and took possession of the sword; also how Merlin, the enchanter, was assotted by the lady of the lake. The amours of Guinevere with Lancelot and of La Belle Ysoude with Tristram are here related; also the various achievements of Lancelot, Tristram, Lamoracke, Gawain,

THE SUPERNATURAL IN ROMANTIC FICTION

Galahad, and others. Some say that Arthur was changed into a raven; others that he was carried away to Avilion, or Avalon. It is supposed that he will one day reappear on earth. A story about him in Scott's "Bridal of Triermain" is simply an old Northern legend adopted and adapted. The sangreal was the vessel containing the blood of Christ, which was collected by Joseph of Arimathea. It was the great object of the Knights of the Round Table to obtain this vessel; and an empty seat, called the perilous siege, was reserved for the knight who should obtain it. Percival and Galahad are the knights particularly connected with the achievement of this adventure. According to one legend, the sangreal was made out of a diamond that fell from the crown of Satan in his combat with Michael. Tristram one of the most celebrated of the Knights of the Round Table, intrigued with Yseult, Ysoude, Iseult, or Isolda, as she is variously called, the wife of King Mark of Cornwall. There are many accounts of the death of Tristram, but the common account is that he was assassinated by King Mark. According to one story, after the death of Tristram, a flower grew out of his grave, and descended into the grave of Yseult. It may be remembered that this miracle is not uncommon in old ballads. King Mark tested the fidelity of his wife by making her drink out of a magic drinking cup. If she had been unfaithful she could not drink without spilling the liquor. Yseult drank, and spilled the liquor unmistakably.

Concerning Gawain the story is that his strength was greater at certain hours of the day than at others. Sir Yvain, or Owen, was a knight of the Round Table who was constantly attended by a tame lion, which proved itself rather a formidable antagonist of the knight's enemies. It will be remembered that Una, the virgin in Spenser's "Faerie Queen" was similarly attended. Ysaie le Triste was the son of Tristam and Yseult He was educated by a hermit in a forest, and was looked after by the fairies. It was Merlin, when imprisoned in the bush, who had requested the fairies to take care of the child. When Ysaie became a man, the fairies gave to him a misshapen dwarf, called Tronc, to be his attendant. This dwarf, condemned to do penance for a while for his misdeeds under this form, is afterwards restored to his better shape and name as the fairy Oberon, son of Julius Caesar and Morgana la Faye. In the history of Huon of Bordeaux, who was one of the paladins of Charlemagne, the fairy Oberon acts a principal part, presenting the knight with the magic horn, that makes the bad dance, and with the magic goblet, that spontaneously fills with wine in the hands of a good man. Much concerning these two knights, Ysaie and Huon, may be found in Dunlop's "History of Fiction."

The other celebrated paladins of Charlemagne, besides Huon, have already been mentioned. Most of them figure in the poems of Boiardo and Ariosto. Among other heroes of these poems is Ruggiero. He was the betrothed of Bradamante, and, mounted on the hippogryph, he reached the magic island of Alcina, a modern Circe, who, after making lovers of men, transformed them to plants and beasts. He, like others, became the paramour of Alcina, until he discovered that her beauty was the effect of enchantment. When Angelica was exposed to a sea-monster, she was rescued by Ruggiero on the hippogryph, in evident imitation of the story of Andromeda and her rescue by Perseus. Astolpho is another hero of the "Orlando Innamorato" and "Orlando Furioso." He was changed into a myrtle by Alcina, and delivered from enchantment by Ruggiero. He was in possession of a golden spear, originally the property of Argalia and afterwards of Bradamante, which had the virtue of overthrowing everybody it encountered. He pursued the harpies into hell, rode the hippogryph to the moon, and had other marvelous adventures.

Amadis of Gaul and similar worthies need hardly be mentioned. The Seven Champions of Christendom may also be dismissed without ceremony. The story of Siegfried, in the "Nibelungen Lied" is, with many differences, that of Sigurd. It is somewhat as follows. Siegfried, a hero, who had acquired the Nibelungen treasure, and had likewise made himself invulnerable, except in one place, by bathing in the blood of a dragon which he had killed, determined to win Kriemhild, sister of Gunther, king of the Burgundians. Gunther himself was desirous of possessing Brunhild, an Amazonian princess, who fought with her suitors, and beheaded them, when she had conquered them. Gunther promised Kriemhild to Siegfried on condition that Siegfried should assist him to conquer Brunhild; who was conquered chiefly by means of a magic garment, which caused Siegfried to be invisible, whilst he rendered aid to Gunther.

Siegfried then married Kriemhild, and Gunther married Brunhild. Siegfried, in helping Gunther to win Brunhild, had taken a ring from her, and given it to his own wife. Kriemhild, in a dispute with Brunhild, shewed her this ring, and reproached her with having been the concubine of Siegfried. This insult Brunhild avenged by persuading her husband Gunther to foully slay his friend and brother-in-law, by stabbing him in the only part where he was vulnerable. With this the first division of the poem ends; the second is decidedly uninteresting. Of the Cid it is narrated that, as the corpse of that Spanish hero was lying in state, a Jew thought to pull its beard. No sooner, however, had he approached for this purpose than the corpse put its hand to its sword. This miracle had a good effect upon the Jew, since he immediately became a Christian. Rustam is the great hero of Eastern romance. His combat with Asfendiar lasted two days. He was a conqueror of the Divs. A Div, named Asdiv, stole upon him in the shape of a dragon, whilst he slept. Rustam was awakened by his horse, and slew his enemy. Tahmuras was a Persian hero, who, mounted on the Simurgh, conquered the Divs, and rescued the Peri Merjan.

THE SUPERNATURAL IN ROMANTIC FICTION

SUPERNATURAL POWERS OF BODY

When Orlando was dying, betrayed by Ganelon at Roncevaux, he sounded, and, in the effort, burst his horn; but so loud was the blast that Charlemagne heard him, although at a distance of sixteen leagues. Like the classical heroes, the heroes of romance often took a scurvy advantage of their opponents by being invulnerable, or by possessing supernatural power. Orlando was invulnerable; Siegfried was nearly so; and the strength of Gawain increased supernaturally at certain hours of the day. The fairies sometimes endowed a man with the strength of twelve men. The gift was occasionally accompanied by the awkward addition of an equal appetite. There is a story, told in different ways, of a hero, who was helped in his adventures by several companions of marvelous capacities. The hearing of one was so fine that he could hear the slightest noise that was made miles away; another could run with incredible speed; another could blow an army away; another could bear enormous loads on his back; and the remaining two had astonishing powers of eating and drinking.

INVISIBILITY

Supernatural beings, like the old gods, are often endowed with invisibility, and can sometimes confer that advantage on those whom they patronize. Bodin, in his "Demonomanie," tells of a person, who was protected by a spirit, generally invisible, which he once saw in the shape of a sleeping child. Fairies are often invisible. One of the elfin princesses in a story by Andersen has the power of vanishing by putting a wand in her mouth. In the "Mort d'Arthur," there is a knight who rides invisible; and many are the stories in which, by wearing a cap or a ring, people have this power of becoming invisible at will. In Shakespeare, and elsewhere, fern-seed is mentioned as a plant that gives invisibility. Ariel and Puck, in common with most other spirits, have this power of making themselves invisible, as well as that of transforming themselves to other shapes. Ghosts are at one time visible, at another time invisible: they may also be visible to one person, whilst invisible to another person. So Hecate was seen only by dogs; and the Furies were visible to the tormented Orestes, whilst invisible to others. Places are at times invisible, as has been shown elsewhere. It has been related of a haunted battle-field that all the sounds of the battle, such as the clashing of arms and the neighing of horses, have been reproduced, whilst nothing of the combat could be seen.

In addition to invisibility, a being may be inaudible to all, except the person he is addressing, as is an angel in one of Calderon's plays.

SUPERNATURAL REVEALMENT

When Asmodeus showed to Don Cleofas the secrets of Madrid, he took, or appeared to take, all the roofs of the houses off. There are many fairy stories, in which the fairies are made by supernatural means to appear as they are, and not in their ordinary invisible or disguised condition. There are also divers stories in which enchanters show by magical mirrors the true reflection of absent persons and things. The "Leech of Folkstone," in the "Ingoldsby Legends" is a very pleasant narrative concerning magic mirrors, but it is not original. Many are the stories wherein by supernatural means hidden riches are revealed. In the "Arabian Nights" Baba Abdallah anoints his eye with a magic ointment, and sees all the concealed treasures of the earth.

IMMOBILITY

The hand of glory is the hand of a man that has been hanged, and is chiefly efficacious in depriving of motion those against whom its power is directed. In the story of the "King of

THE SUPERNATURAL IN ROMANTIC FICTION

the Black Islands" in the "Arabian Nights," the king is permanently fixed to his couch through the magic of his wife, who changes the lower half of him to marble. A story, to be found in Keightley's "Fairy Mythology," tells how a giant was changed to stone, and only temporarily recovered animation for one day in each year. Prospero exercises his magical power on Ferdinand, and apparently makes him motionless:

> Thy nerves are in their infancy again,
> And have no power in them.

Comus sets the lady in an enchanted chair, where she is obliged to sit "In stony fetters, fixed and motionless."

ENLARGEMENT AND DIMINUTION

Among other powers usually possessed by supernatural beings is that of accommodating their size to circumstances. In "Paradise Lost," we find the devils diminishing themselves. In the Hindu fables Hanuman enlarges or reduces himself at will. In a story by Hauff, an angry dwarf becomes a giant. Witches too must reduce themselves very much in size before they can go in and out of auger-holes, and swim in egg-shells and sieves. In "Faust" the poodle swells to the size of an elephant before finally adjusting itself to the form of a student. Moses in the Turkish story is by divine power enlarged to the dimensions of a giant. An instance of diminution, or rather of marvelous compression, is in the story where the Troll encloses a lake in a letter. The letter is opened, the water rushes out, and converts a valley into a lake.

SUPERNATURAL TRAVELS

In "Hassan of Balsora," as well as in much other Oriental fiction, the traveling is of a very marvelous sort. In the Swedish story, similar to "Hassan of Balsora," a youth seeks a

THE SUPERNATURAL IN ROMANTIC FICTION

fairy princess, who has fled away in the form of a bird, but has first told him that she dwells in the beautiful palace that lies beyond the sun. He accomplishes part of the journey to her residence in boots that go a hundred miles at every step, and does the rest on the back of a phoenix. The travels of Sindbad and Aboulfaouris are full of the supernatural. Aboulfaouris was carried away by the Jinn to a place which was, according to the rate of human traveling, ninety years' journey from his home. Mounted, however, on the back of an Afreet, he might be conveyed thither in three hours. Cyrano de Bergerac wrote concerning expeditions to the moon and to the sun. Swift, in his "Gulliver's Travels" and Voltaire, in his "Micromegas" seem to have taken hints from the work of Cyrano, who, in his turn, may have borrowed from Lucian. These productions of Swift and Voltaire are vehicles for satire and philosophy, and have little to do with fancy. Edgar Poe in a story, which he wrote concerning a voyage to the moon, seems to show an acquaintance with Cyrano. Pultock's "Peter Wilkins," which may be considered an imitation of "Gulliver" as well as of "Robinson Crusoe" and of the "Arabian Nights" is but a poor production. Fielding has written a story in which the travels of a soul after death are narrated.

THE SUPERNATURAL IN ALLEGORY

As an example of the above may be quoted the following Oriental parable, which is to be found in the Greek romance of "Josaphat and Barlaam." A man, flying from an unicorn, by which he was pursued, had nearly fallen into a deep pit, but saved himself by grasping the twigs of a slender shrub, which grew on the side. While he hung suspended over the abyss by this feeble hold, he observed two mice, the one white and the other black, gnawing the root of the plant to which he had trusted. At the bottom of the gulf was a monstrous dragon, breathing forth flames, and prepared to devour him; while by this time the unicorn was looking at him over the verge of the pit; In this situation he perceived honey distilling from the branches to which he was clinging, and, unmindful of the horrors by which he was surrounded, he satiated himself with the sweets, which were dropping from the boughs. Here the unicorn is Death, by which all men are pursued; the pit is the World, full of evils; the shrub, of which the root was corroded by the white and black mice, is Life, diminished, and at length consumed by Day and Night; the dragon is Hell, and the honey Pleasure.

The comparison of Night and Day to a black animal and a white one is common enough. In the "Turkish Stories." Night and Day are compared to a black sheep and a white one, which are perpetually chasing one another. The simile has been repeated in modern poetry. Bunyan's "Pilgrim's Progress" is among the most celebrated allegorical works. Christian wades through the slough of Despond, fights with Apollyon, passes successfully the cave of the giants Pagan and Pope. It is, however, hardly necessary to accompany him further on his adventures. The "Faerie Queen" is as thorough a specimen of the allegorical poem as may well be. It is, as its author says, a continued allegory. In the Faerie Queen herself he allegorises both Glory and Queen Elizabeth. The Red Cross Knight, as Holiness, slays the monster Error, and comes to a house, where Pride, Vanity, Gluttony and the rest are personified. Sir Guyon, or Temperance, enters the cave of Mammon, where Care guards the treasures of the god, and where Ambition sits, holding a golden chain, which reaches from heaven to hell. The Blatant Beast is an allegorical monster, representing Censure or Calumny. According to the modern wise men, such as Professors Max Muller and de Gubernatis, most, if not all, of the beautiful old stories are simply allegorical, and may be explained by natural phenomena, such as the rising and the setting of the sun. They may be right, but one would rather not believe so. The explanation makes the old stories somewhat uninteresting. In the "Ruins" of Volney the Christian religion is treated in the same way, and is explained as a solar myth.

THE SUPERNATURAL IN ROMANTIC FICTION

SUPERNATURAL CONCEITS

In "Abdallah," a book to be found in the "Cabinet des Fees," there is a story, in which a princess is conveyed to a world where all things are the reverse of what they are in this world. There the old are young; the young are old. Fleas are as large as our elephants, and elephants as small as our fleas. The forests are composed of blades of grass; the herbage of diminutive forests. Of these and similar fatiguing absurdities does the story consist. Cyrano de Bergerac's account of voyages to the moon and sun, whilst aiming at satire, is for the most part made up of conceits of this sort.

The same may be said to a certain extent of "Gulliver's Travels." This, however, being a powerful work, the conceits are interesting. Moreover, satire underlies the whole narrative. The Limbo, or Paradise of Fools, with its contents, as described by Milton, may certainly be considered whimsical. The fictions of Baron Munchausen are very extravagant, but have no real invention or humor. One does not see why a poet, like Burger, should have condescended to translate such rubbish. Whatever else may be good in Rabelais, the supernatural extravagance is bad. As an instance of its monstrous incongruity, Pantagruel, a giant so huge that a nation resides within his mouth, is nevertheless the lover of a Parisian lady.

THE SUPERNATURAL IN FABLE

The following is the substance of a fable by Bidpai. A man picked up a mouse, took it home, and prayed God to change it into a girl, which transformation was accordingly effected. Some years after, he told her to choose a husband. She chose the most powerful being in creation, whoever that might be. The man, thereupon, addressed the Sun, thinking that to be the mightiest being. But the Sun modestly replied that the Cloud, which obscured his light, was more powerful. The Cloud, on appeal being made to it, acknowledged itself inferior to the Wind, which could disperse it. The Wind admitted the superiority of the Mountain, which could arrest its progress. The Mountain said that the Rat was stronger than itself, since it could pierce its sides, and enter it at will. So the girl was engaged to marry the Rat; but, in order to make the match more equal, it was thought better to transform her back into a Mouse; which was done. There is a fable, attributed to Aesop, which is similar to many old fairy-stories, in which greed is punished, and honesty, or civility, rewarded.

One instance of these stories is that, versified by Parnell, where a good fellow accidentally falls in with the fairies, and has the hump on his back taken off; and a bad fellow, hearing of this, intentionally meets with the fairies, with the purpose of being rewarded, but, betraying his right disposition, gets nothing but the hump of the other man placed permanently on his own back. The probably spurious fable of Aesop is this. A woodman loses his hatchet in a stream. Mercury appears to him with a golden hatchet, and asks him whether it is his. The man says No. Mercury then shows him a silver hatchet. The man still says No. Mercury then restores him the lost hatchet, and, as a reward for his honesty, gives him also the other two. A companion of the man, hearing the story, goes to the stream, and designedly loses his hatchet. The god appears, as before, with the golden hatchet, which the man claims. The god is disgusted with his greediness, and, far from giving him another hatchet, will not allow him to have even his own again.

THE END